DayBook for New Voices

DayBook for New Voices

A Calendar of
Reflections and Prayers
by and for Youth

EDITED BY MAREN C. TIRABASSI AND MARIA I. TIRABASSI

Presented to

Participants of United Church of Christ National Youth Event 2004

As a gift from

LOCAL CHURCH MINISTRIES
Rev. José A. Malayang, Executive Minister

WORSHIP AND EDUCATION MINISTRY TEAM
Rev. José Abraham De Jesús, Team Leader
Rev. June Boutwell, Youth, Young Adult and Outdoor Ministries

THE PILGRIM PRESS
Rev. Timothy G. Staveteig, Publisher

with an attitude of great thanksgiving for the gifts and faithfulness of young people
who continue to embrace, enlighten, encourage, and empower the church as they
seek God's vision, follow Christ's call, and are led by the Spirit.

THE PILGRIM PRESS   CLEVELAND

The Pilgrim Press, 700 Prospect Avenue, Cleveland, Ohio 44115-1100
thepilgrimpress.com
Copyright © 2004 by Maren C. Tirabassi and Maria I. Tirabassi

09   08   07   06   05   04   5   4   3   2   1

Library of Congress Cataloging-in-Publication Data
Daybook for new voices : a calendar of reflections and prayers by and for youth /
  edited by Maren C. Tirabassi and Maria I. Tirabassi.
    p. cm.
    Includes index.
    ISBN 0-8298-1603-8 (pbk. : alk. paper)
    1. Youth—Prayer-books and devotions—English.   2. Devotional calendars.
  I. Tirabassi, Maren C. II. Tirabassi, Maria I., 1983–

BV4850.D38 2004
242'.83—dc22

2004049414

CONTENTS

Introduction

MORNING — Waking Up or the Essence of this Book

The DayBook for New Voices is a project that floated on conversations over countless cups of English breakfast tea taken with milk and, in my case, a liberal helping of sugar, during face-to-face conversations and then, in the autumn when I returned to college, over the telephone and Internet. My mother and I had responded enthusiastically to June Boutwell's suggestion to follow up on Mom's first book of this kind, *Blessing New Voices,* in advance of the 2004 National Youth Event. My mother began by getting the word out to past youth contributors, churches, youth groups, and schools. I was fortunate enough to be given the opportunity to travel to General Synod in Minneapolis, Minnesota, where I met young people so empowered and excited by their faith and our invitation to write it, that I was reminded that my own relationship with God needed tending. As we began to read the words tentatively or boldly submitted to us over the months, this desire awakened again and again, and our concept started stirring—becoming a book far brighter than we could possibly have imagined.

Our daily prayer idea, which we first thought to be straightforward and practical, has evolved into a collection of writings that allows young people to speak out to God, each other, and adults across the boundaries of age, gender, and religious convictions. Here are the cries and rejoicings of a group too seldom heard in faith communities. Here is a generation longing to share passion, hope, and confusion—the very foundations of the adolescent experience—a generation longing to be heard, but also to hear the words of God and earth mingling together on every tongue. Here is a book that celebrates the fervor of youth written by experts on the subject—the youth, themselves.

We hope that everyone who picks up this book appreciates the suffering and elation of the most common human experience—growth—and in doing so, recalls the difficulties that accompany it. We realize there will be different memories, experiences, and understandings for each person, and we ask every reader to come with an open heart, willing to engage and be challenged by the ideas of these young adults—peers or not. Please accept this offering from my mother, myself, and many amazing writers. We hope you enjoy it.

—*Maria I. Tirabassi*

AFTERNOON — How to Use This Book

The DayBook for New Voices includes a prayer, poem, or reflection for every day of the year. Following a year by using this book would be a particularly wonderful way for adults to listen to the views and hopes of young people. Often the voices of youth are segregated to Youth Sunday, Children's Day, a mission trip report, or Baccalaureate. Taking a few minutes every day of the year with the words of young people would be a deepening spiritual practice. Printing one of the prayers for the week in a Sunday bulletin would open up a congregation. Young people themselves may be interested in following the seasons this way during their confirmation year or in the year following confirmation.

It is also possible to read through the *DayBook* continuously like a single volume of poems, prayers, and reflections or skip around through the text, focusing on different issues or concerns. The seasonal scope is broad. Because many holidays change in date, readers will find prayers throughout the month in which a celebration or season falls. Reflections about mothers are found in May; thanksgiving prayers predominate in November. Lenten pieces appear in both March and April, while camp-related writings are scattered through the summer. Some single dates received multiple submissions—look through all of February for romantic love, July for patriotism, September for thoughts and feelings about September 11, 2001.

There are six additions each month to the writings of young people. We decided to broaden the book's perspective by soliciting prayers and reflections from adults who work with young people (youth leaders, coaches, pastors, high school teachers, a juvenile detention counselor, a movie theatre manager, etc.) and parents. The adult contributions occur on the seventh, fourteenth, twenty-first, and twenty-eighth of each month (with holiday exceptions and a couple extras).

In each month there are also two biblical reflections. On the sixteenth an adolescent character in the Bible is spotlighted. These twelve Bible studies consist of a text, three questions for personal reflection or even discussion in a youth group or confirmation class, and a short prayer. On the fifth of each month there is a "Pause for Psalms." The psalms chosen are some less common ones that display strong emotions, and the reader is invited to reflect on these emotions by entering into the psalm and then writing a psalm that is closely or loosely based on the feelings of these texts so ancient but so realistic even for today. An example is given each time, but the hope is that teenagers and adults who are reading will stretch their own creativity.

The *DayBook* is a book for reading, but it is also a book for writing! In these pages are acrostics, haiku, a baccalaureate invocation, poems dedicated to dearly loved friends, living and dead, an irate letter to God, litanies for holiday celebrations, a group prayer before an AIDS walk, several reflections on the SATs and one on working in a video store, passionate cries for God's healing, and carefully crafted descriptions of seasonal beauty. The book is intended not only to reflect the thoughts of nearly three hundred writers, but to jump-start others to put into words their hopes, longings, doubts, fears, dreams . . . all of which are received by God as prayer.

—*Maren C. Tirabassi*

EVENING — Some Folks We Include in Our Bedtime Prayers!

We wish to express thanks to many who have made this book a reality. Writers, writers, writers!

We are deeply grateful to young people from across the United States, ranging in age from twelve to twenty-one (with five exceptions, two younger and three older) who trusted us with their thoughtful words. The largest group are members of the United Church of Christ but there are also representatives of a wide variety of Protestant denominations and the Roman Catholic and Greek Orthodox traditions. Many contributors did not identify their faith community, but we are aware of Jewish, Muslim, Taoist, and Wiccin participants. The book includes broad ethnic and racial diversity, different sexual orientations, both rural and urban community settings, and a variety of economic and educational backgrounds. The age dispersion is fairly even with a slight weight to the older end of the spectrum. College students and working young adults are a significant presence that was missing in the earlier book, *Blessing New Voices*. By the end of the process every region of the country was very well represented. Thank you, writers.

We also appreciate the adult contributors, who were solicited later in the process, after we decided to expand the project, and who promptly and wonderfully offered their heartfelt words.

In the last weeks of the project we realized that some of the original correspondents were not going to return their permissions for publication, and we received help from a very special group of young people—who may not have come from the lanes and hedgerows, but certainly responded to our "banquet invitation" to spend some of their Christmas vacation writing replacement prayers. Thanks to Greg, Carlie, Sam, Shannon, Bithy, Stephanie, Sarah, Olin, Courtney, Aaron, Emilie, the two Matts, and Jeannine.

Among many youth leaders who encouraged their group members to submit to the book, there were some leaders and pastors who were shepherds for large groups through the entire process, from prayer writing workshops to permission letters. Kudos to Cheryl Bright, Mahalia Clark, Kris Snyder-Samuelson, Nancy Fowler, David Pendleton, Pam Spain, Chris Hanson, Diane and Kevin Hollander, Mary Kernander, Betsey Natale, Carl McDonald, and Megan Weymouth. Everyone should have a pastor like Scott Martin.

This follow-up volume to *Blessing New Voices* is the the brain-child of June Boutwell, Minister for Youth, Young Adults and Outdoors Ministries, and we appreciate her vision and her many forms of practical assistance. Her sponsorship of Maria at General Synod in Minneapolis as well as the support from the members of Youth, Young Adults and Outdoors Ministries there gave a helpful early impetus to this project. Collaborating with her is Timothy Staveteig, our publisher, for whose guidance and advice we are deeply grateful. Kimberlee Nagy-Bublik and the wonderful staff of The Pilgrim Press continue to make our tasks so much easier.

Finally, no project like this can come to life without personal support, patience, and a certain amount of hand-holding and technical assistance, and so we are deeply grateful to Aaron Farber and Donald Tirabassi.

— Maren and Maria Tirabassi

January

JANUARY 1

Lying out
Spread eagle on the crisp, cold snow.
Frozen crystals poking
Their edges sharp through my thick wool hat,
Damp after a night on the ice.
The sky a collage of stars
Framed by naked, knotted branches,
A gnarled set of arms embracing the full sky.
Its mirage playing on the sleek ice
Painted black by the heavy brush of night
A mirror image of heaven,
Stretching out across the smooth ice
Ending at the edge of the pond.
The beginning of the snowy, mortal world
Where I lay looking up.

Ashley Martin

JANUARY 2

In January we ring in the New Year
with intended resolutions wrapped in bright cheer.
Most of our goals are for slimmer waists,
fitter bodies and healthier tastes.
But what we often fail to exercise most
is our fitness of Spirit in the Holy Ghost!

In the month of new starts,
May we keep God close to our hearts.

Allison Wroe

JANUARY 3

A new year for PKs

It's really something special to belong
at Christmas.

I never appreciated it
until there were no familiar faces
in the pews around me.

I never understood
that belonging
is part of the God-ness.

I always took for granted
those people who made holiness
something I could hold on to.

For a preacher's kid,
not belonging at Christmas
is like forgetting that God

is me.

JANUARY 4

Sliding in the snow

Do you remember last winter when the snow banks were white? God, you made the hills so perfect for sliding. We went so fast in that sparkling snow. The pine trees whiz by with a blur of green and the smell of pine. My friends and I enjoy this time in the nice clean fields that you made for us. Amen.

Sanne Brown

JANUARY 5

Pause for Psalms—Psalm 84

Read Psalm 84.

What is the mood or tone of this psalm? What feelings are expressed? Do you understand the person who wrote this psalm? Can you identify a popular song, movie, or television show in which these emotions are explored? Choose a single verse or line from this psalm and spend some quiet time reflecting on it . . . or simply repeat it over and over again. Create your own words for this psalm. Here is one contemporizing of it.

Psalm 84

Nest me in the corners of your love—
make me sparrow
in the shelter
of your heart,
and, when I swallow-fly
to far-lonely heights,
let me fold my wings into you.

Hire me as the keeper of your doors—
not to close
but to open them wide
to every wandering soul
in the storms of life . . .
let me guide them in
to your home.

JANUARY 6

Lord, in times when all seems to be lost
you hold our heads up and give us strength.

When the world is but a masquerade
you open our eyes to the truth behind.

When words seem to rust and blow away
you catch them and show us their radiance.

When pain bogs us down and buries us
you are there to see us through.

When loneliness tears at our hearts and minds
you give us friends and love.

And when there is death and despair
you show us the light at the end of the tunnel.

Lord, for strength, for truth, for radiance, for
guidance, for friends, for love, and for light
We thank you, Lord. Amen.

Jonathan Bush

JANUARY 7

Prayer of the Attentive Heart

There are times, Father,
    when my hand falters, unsure of the next move.
        As I loosen my grasp on all I have known,
           I feel your warm touch,
guiding my fingers to a course untried,
    and I am led onward . . .

             May I so do for Others.

There are times, Father,
    when I long to *just stop!* To stop doing,
        stop running, stop falling behind,
           stop catching up.
To be still, be fed, be carried, be led,
    be lifted, listened to,
        be loved, believed,
           to just BE.

        Always you have been there,
           waiting in the still, welcoming my embrace . . .

             May I so be for Others.

Margaret Chamberlain (adult)

JANUARY 8

School Issues

O God, please help me get through the seventh grade again. When I found out that I had to stay back I hated you because I didn't like the fact that I had to go through the same grade as my little sister. But now I understand why you held me back. I understand why you held me back because everything in my life was going wrong with the friends I had, and now I am glad you helped me through all that. I am glad you are helping me through all of this pain and trouble I am going through.

Samantha Benson

JANUARY 9

They come and go, these chess pieces of life.
Of course, the position of King
is none other than yours, master of your domain,
and the rooks, knights, and pawns are taken by life's opposing pieces.

There's always that one piece you can rely on though—
your shining beacon, the Queen to your King—
your ultimate protection in the darkness of night,
your true hope and faith.
I know my Queen and even though she can't always be directly by my side,
she continues to be my protector—
my shining beacon.

Shannon Glaser

JANUARY 10

Dear God, help the homeless and the needy. Help those who need to get
homes and food. Help those who need to stay warm and cozy. Also, please
help the innocent stay safe from danger. Keep our troops safe in Iraq and in
Afghanistan. Thank you, and please keep us safe. Amen.

Travis Turnbough

JANUARY 11

Now Is the Time

He is my brother
I am their daughter
We are all children
We should work together
Now is the time
We can make the difference
Show the world that we care
Show them there is hope here
Don't waste a moment
Know what you're all about

Remember, in the end,
Only love will remain.

Annie Lalish

JANUARY 12

Hey God,
How are you? I'm doing OK. I know that, for me, you have been true to
your word and have been there for me in times of need or just when I felt
like talking. It is hard to believe that I cannot see you, touch you, or know
that you are really there, but you are still such a big part of my life. You
give me strength and the will to do things I never thought I could do. My
faith in you helps me through each day, good and bad, because I know you
will always be there to listen and that you will never judge me or lose faith
in me if I do something wrong. You guide me through life year after year
and I know that you will never leave my side. You will always be the only
true and constant thing in my life. You are the one thing that I know I can
go back to for guidance and reassurance. I thank you for giving your only
son, so that I may live. Lastly, I thank you for my friends and family who
support me each day and for keeping all of us safe and protected. In Jesus'
name I pray.

Seana Clark

JANUARY 13

Winter is coming soon, which means that basketball season is near.
The sweet sound of dribbling and the ball swishing through the net.
All the determination in players' eyes and only winning on their minds.
As the pressure mounts higher, the team works harder together.
Thank you, God, for letting me be able to play basketball.
I pray the season will never end.

Kyle Bailey

JANUARY 14

O God

My anxieties overwhelm me
     My fears paralyze me.
   My addiction is my only safe place
Even while I know it is killing me I can at least count on it,
     depend on it for a few moments
        to lift the clawing darkness that aches in my chest.

I need something else
I know I do

But the "hospitals for the soul"
Put their doctors on trial
   Attack their "wounded healers" with a savagery that makes Salem and
      McCarthy seem tame.
They aren't safe places any more.
Even while they sing
"O Come, O Come, Emanuel, and ransom captive Israel"
   no real captives need apply.

I don't need
Sanitized shepherds with "Downy soft" sheep
Angels that can be tethered to a northern pine

I need the terrifying news
That you are here
in the sweat and the blood and the manure.
In the rush of wings
that stops the human breath and heart;
   in a high clearer and sharper,
      warmer and more penetrating
than any drug;
   in an ecstasy beyond any orgasm;
in a healing homecoming that will make me whole.

It's Christmas
   And I'm lost out in life's field
     I'm lonely, and cold, and afraid.
Show me where the stable is.

Stephen Price (adult)

JANUARY 15

Not all dreams involve being naked in math class

I have a dream
to belong

I have a dream
to help others belong

I have a dream
to keep those who belong from frowning on those who do not

I have a dream
to keep there from being any who do not belong

I have a dream
to belong

JANUARY 16

Bible Study—Jairus's Daughter

Read Mark 5:21–24, 35–43.

1) Parents are often desperate for physical, psychological, and/or emotional healing for their children. Have you seen this in your own family or others?

2) What kills twelve-year-old girls in these days? (The fact that Jesus told the parents to give her something to eat may be suggestive.)

3) What friends of yours do you hope Jesus heals in some way?

PRAYER: God, bring healing and hope to these people who are in such a difficult situation that even their parents or particularly their parents cannot help: _____ . Let me be your disciple, even by "raising the dead." Amen.

JANUARY 17

God,

It's awful to feel excluded because of my faith. When I enter into other churches and they say I don't belong because I hold different beliefs, I question the strength of love between people. I want to be able to proclaim that we are all one, regardless of the nature of our faith, the color of our skin, the country of our birth, or the language that we speak, but I know that I do not live in a perfect world. There are too many people who cannot accept who I am and the choices I've made, and there are too few who choose to join with me to promote understanding.

God, I want to believe in the innate goodness of all people, but sometimes it's hard when those I should look up to are teaching lessons of hatred and intolerance toward others. I don't always know where to turn when I've been slighted, when I've been hurt, when praying doesn't seem to be enough to stop the pain; I don't even know how to reach people or how to explain to them that they've hurt me.

How can I go on trying to teach love and compassion when so many seem bent on destruction? When will I know that my work has been worthy, that my struggling has not been in vain? Where should I look to see compassionate understanding if I can't look to those who are supposed to be leading me?

Teach me, God, to understand love on the smallest level so that I won't be discouraged when the bigger picture gets blurred. Help me to see once more the goodness that can and does exist in all of my sisters and brothers around the world. Don't let me lose faith, God, when I know you still believe in us and in all we are capable of doing.
Shalom.

Anonymous, Cambridge, Massachusetts

JANUARY 18

The strength

I sit on the bus as my team laughs and cheers,
Thinking about the game and every aspect,
Listening to my favorite CD, I get in the mode of the game.
The beat of the music soothes my soul, so that I may think about the game
    that I will be playing.

I pray that, as the captains, Meagan and I lead our team to a victory.
I pray that my team can be a whole.
I pray that Courtney, Jackie, and Sam have a great setting game.
I pray that Ashley and Nicky have the strength to use their voices.
I pray that Rachel L. and Rachel S. have the strength to spike that ball.
I pray that Brittany and Becky have the strength to Ace!
I pray that Andrea has the strength to serve and bump that ball.
Amen.

Chantale Lyons

JANUARY 19

Dear God,
How could you come up with this dead but beautiful season called winter.
The wonderful snow that comes from the sky is a beautiful, magical thing.
It transforms my front lawn into a wonderland, covered in a white blanket.
The cool crisp air that whips by my head gives me chills and a pink colored
face. I love the sports that this season offers, like skiing, skating, and sled-
ding. I thank you for all the wonderful things that this season brings me.
Amen.

Taylor Renaud

JANUARY 20

Confirmation class creed

As brothers and sisters in faith, we believe that God is like a flashlight that
shines the way through the darkest paths in life. When life leads us off the
road, he is there to guide us back. God is our protector who guards us from
evil. God has created the world and all that is in it. God calls us to love
him and one another.

We believe Jesus Christ is the path to eternal life. He died for our sins so
that we may be forgiven. Endowed with the power of God, Jesus shows us
the way to lead our lives. He is the key we need to open the gates of
heaven. "What Would Jesus Do?" is the question that governs our lives.
Jesus is our role model, our teacher, our friend, and our Savior.

We believe that the Holy Spirit is the eternal flame of God's love, burning in each of us. Without the Holy Spirit our lives would be meaningless. We believe that when we invite the Holy Spirit into our lives we are asking God to help us whenever we are in distress. The Holy Spirit is God alive in us.

We believe the church is a meeting place for all believers of God to come together and praise him. In the church we can build our relationships with God, Jesus Christ, the Holy Spirit, and other people. We believe the Bible is the word of God, which tells the good deeds God has done. If you believe in God and follow the Bible, you will never become lost.

This is the faith we seek to live. Thanks be to God! Amen.
St. Peter's Evangelical Church, UCC, Ferguson, Missouri

Kevin Crutcher, Michael Cooper, Garrett Hemann, Mary Hoemeyer,
Matthew Hundelt, Aaron Kirchhoff, Meghan Krato, Robbie Yakel

JANUARY 21

Prayer of a parent about food

Dear God, we pray for the anorexics and bulimics,
for young people, especially women
who seek to be small and in control,
who long for an image which can never be met.
We pray for young men who use steroids,
who exercise and struggle
with unachievable proportions.
We pray for young adults who are overweight
and suffer the scorns of a society
which is so consumed by slender and sexy.
We pray for families where food is a battleground—
vegetarian or vegan verses meat-eating,
love identified with food, dangerous diets.
We pray for grace, even as we pray "grace" at our tables.
Give us this day our daily bread . . . of love. Amen.

JANUARY 22

Dear God,
Winter is my favorite season.
Snow boarding, skiing, having snowball fights, building snow caves, sliding, and playing ice hockey all make winter the best. Snow days are fun because there is no school. It's fun to play in the snow and have friends over. Winter is the best, God. Good idea!

Chris Brown

JANUARY 23

Revealing

Don't tell me I'm pretty; don't tell me I'm sexy—
it only makes it hurt more
because you don't mean it.
I'm just me: I'm smart, I'm perverted, I think
too much, I can't tell a joke, I am too serious.
Don't make me tell you
the truth.
It strains and cracks my voice, I feel
like crying or running away
to hide.
It hurts to pull out the words like pulling a rope out
of my throat.
It breaks it tears seams my rusty
hinges groan creaking boards in dark
lonely house where no one is allowed too
much weight disturbs dust don't
push too hard.
It reveals scars and opens wounds it opens
me I can't tell you I can't show you
me real me.
What's the point I don't
have a chance with you
anyway.
I want it so badly I want to be held and
warm and loved and petted and kissed and

talked to listened to valued
touched.
I feel hard cold why am I untouchable
of course I don't won't can't
let anyone in.
I want to be attractive am I not because
I am not or because I am convinced
I am not?
I watch the dating game go
round and round when is
my turn?
Spin me around on that wild and crazy
ride let me fly if only
to fall I'd rather fall than feel
held down.

Gabriele S. Chase

JANUARY 24

Share with others.
Find somebody to interest yourself in.
Share with him or her your love . . .
of life, of love, of sunlight, of dark.

Find a passion to share and exert that love—
show it to another person, and find out
how they can love it, too.

Olin Johannessen

JANUARY 25

All across town it is snowing.
The moon is reflecting on the snow.
I can see it out my window.
I hope I fall asleep soon
so I can go outside and play.
Thank you, God, for the snow
to make snow-families.
Thank you for the ice to skate on.

Amanda Bolstridge

JANUARY 26

Statement of Faith (read antiphonally)

We believe in God, the Eternal Spirit and Jesus Christ.
God, our Eternal Spirit, you are our Savior.
You show us the way of life, God, and give us Holy Love.
You give love to all who follow you.
We look to Jesus Christ, our risen Savior, as our example.
*You have allowed us to create our own image and be followers
of Christ.*
The church shows us joy, passion, and victory.
*You guide us through our eternal life. You help us renew the covenant
of our church.*
God, we promise to trust you, to forgive, to have courage, and to pray for
peace.
You trust all who trust you.
We rejoice because of eternal life. Bless us, for we honor your power and
glory.
*Your forgiveness, presence, and love bless us and honor us as you guide
us in this world.*
Amen.
Amen.

Confirmation Class of 2003
Maple Street Congregational Church, UCC, Danvers, Massachusetts

JANUARY 27

Raise my hand . . . wave good-bye.
Hop on the plane, I'm ready to fly.
Though the journey is long,
let it go without a hitch.
On another continent, another house,
another language and thought.
I let go, until the winds carry me home.

Jeannine Karr

JANUARY 28

Prayer of a parent whose child is going abroad

God, may my child arrive safely at her destination. May the values and
skills she has learned serve her well and help her represent our family and
our nation in the country she is visiting. May her mind and heart be open
to the new ideas and customs that she will observe and discover. May she
make new friends and gain a broader understanding of the family of na-
tions. May she enjoy new sights, new sounds, new foods, new pleasures.
May she miss us and our home and her friends enough to remind her that
she is well-loved . . . but not so much that she will be lonely. And, when she
has shared her talents and ideas with her new friends, and they with her,
may she return to us safely a better person for her experiences. Amen.

Diane Karr

JANUARY 29

Domestic violence. There's nothing domestic about it. It's ugly. It tore my
friend's home apart. I saw them standing in the freezing rain with all their
stuff in a snow bank waiting for the people from the shelter to come pick
them up. I was angry, so angry I could have melted the ice on the windows—the windows through which I was watching, the safe windows.
God—love my neighbor as myself? I wish my neighbors could love each
other. Only you can help. Please help.

Anonymous, Des Moines, Iowa

JANUARY 30

Computer Prayer at Bedtime

God, please let the electrons flow charged
from socket to plug, and
let the cable modem
successfully connect
to the Internet upload and download
without impediment . . .
all four lights shining,
steadily,
all night . . .
Thanks.

Emilie Karr

JANUARY 31

It has taken me a while to get to this point. The point where I feel comfortable speaking to you, the point where I believe you might actually be listening. All I ask is that you stay with me. Help me to always feel your love and never doubt it. I can remember the times when I felt you had abandoned me and that you didn't care, that you didn't really exist. I remember that bitterness and I am grateful for it now. It helps me to realize every day how amazing you are, how incredible and beautiful and precious my faith is to me. I thank you for finding me, and I pray that we never get lost to each other again.

Elizabeth Randell

ROOM FOR YOUR THOUGHTS

February

FEBRUARY 1

A Prayer for Valentine's Day

At a time when so many are rejoicing in their love for one another, let us not forget those who do not have this gift. Keep in our hearts the lonely, the forgotten, the unloved. Help us hold them in our hearts as we hold in our hearts our loved ones. Hold all people in your arms, O God, the content and the happy, the rejected and the wounded; help them to know your love. Fulfill their hearts; bring them a deep love unknown to many on this earth.

Katherine M. Spain

FEBRUARY 2

Free

My feet have been bonded.
I have traveled a great distance.
My hands show the work I have done.
My eyes cry tears of sorrow and longing.
My back is the proof of scars,
Of beatings others and I have been through.
Nights of coldness and darkness
Others can't and didn't bear.
I am here inside my shack,
While he is up there in the grand house,
Nice and warm in his bed.
I'm frozen and broken under my blanket,
Thinking of ways to hide and flee.
He may have taken my dignity and pride,
Yet my soul and will are still mine.
In God I trust to keep me safe,
For when I run away,
Darkness will hide me
And water will wash away my scent.
A slave I may be,
But I'm also a child of God.
To run away from him I must,
To be free of bonds and beatings
Up North through the Underground Railroad.
My future is unknown
Yet my destiny is clear.
Through trials and tribulations,
God will set me free.
Free I will and must be
To do as I wish and please.
So when I leave, do not fret,
For I will die or live;
Either way I will be free.
Free of all the pain I have been through,
Free to be who I am,
Free of another person's rule and will,
Enjoying the freedom I have been longing for,

I will be free.
Free to enjoy life
Free to be my own person
Under my own rule—
Free!

Dave Adkins

FEBRUARY 3

Beauty

Oh God, you could make me the ugliest person in the world and I would still be beautiful inside.

Samantha Benson

FEBRUARY 4

Dear God,
I know you're my number one fan. You're always cheering me on. Now, when I need you most, I'm glad that you'll be there. I want your help in knowing what to do with this boy I met. I think I really like him and I know he loves you, too. I don't want to make the mistakes I've made in the past. I want to love him faithfully, but only with your approval. Sometimes, though, I just can't hear you, so please forgive me. Amen.

Erica Boyer

FEBRUARY 5

Pause for Psalms—Psalm 147

Read Psalm 147.

What is the mood or tone of this psalm? What feelings are expressed? Do you understand the person who wrote this psalm? Can you identify a popular song, movie, or television show in which these emotions are explored? Choose a single verse or line from this psalm and spend some quiet time reflecting on it . . . or simply repeat it over and over again. Create your own words for this psalm. Here is one contemporizing of it.

Psalm 147

Hey, Sirius—here dog-star, here!

Look at the snow—icy-beautiful,
scattered like hoarfrost.
Whoops—just a little melting breath.

Did you say the baby ravens need lunch?
Don't let them cry . . . I'm coming.
Just let me finish with this broken heart.

Peace and wheat—always a good menu
for "happy birthday."
Have some wind, word, wisdom, waters.

Calm down, you horses and athletes.
I need to put Bandaids
on all the hurt children in the world.

Hey, Orion—keep your toys to yourself.

FEBRUARY 6

my soul holds yours close
though our bodies are far apart
your laugh brings me joy
no matter what
we are in the same boat
i dream of your embrace, your form

i finally find you in my dreams
only to have the morning
leave me cold
i refuse to give up
with so many unspoken thoughts
yet i know, in a sense, they
have already been said
'til the day in person
they leave our lips we find
the peace we long for
within the other both willing
to offer protection from this world
no problem too big
no problem too small
always a word of advice
or a hug and kind thought
to see us through
i feel that i am the richest
in this world being able to say
my treasure is you

Katelyn Taylor

FEBRUARY 7

Prayer of a Youth Group Chaperone

God, I want to touch them. I want to hug them when they are sad, hold hands at tender midnight Communion services, put an arm around shoulders after a hard-working day at a mission trip. But these days physical contact is taboo. I recognize how open to misunderstanding touch is, and I know how many sexual and emotional predators are searching for the vulnerable, and I certainly have been well-informed about insurance and litigation.

Still I wish I could touch these teenagers, make that simple body contact that telegraphs love, support, caring, comfort.

God, keep me responsible. Help me stifle my frustrations and not let them leak poison into our program. Stimulate my creativity to give "hugs" with a smile, a compliment, silent nontouching companionship, a written or emailed note of appreciation. Remind me always that praying for someone is the deepest, truest intimacy.

I am praying . . . first for every one of them . . . and also for me. Amen.

FEBRUARY 8

I have loved. I have lost.
I have seen. I have been.
I will stay. I will go.
I will win. I will lose.
But in his eyes I will be one to enter his kingdom come.

Cameron Folden

FEBRUARY 9

Memorial for a Birthday Past

February 9, 2001

On my eighteenth birthday, Chris died from meningitis.
The doctors had misdiagnosed him
and he didn't survive their mistake. I cried
over the cupcakes I had been frosting
and I cried alone under the comforter and I cried
in the middle of a thousand people who turned up to mourn his passing.

He grinned from the yearbook snapshot
blown up and placed next to the pulpit
and I wondered if he was embarrassed
watching all of us from heaven
or wherever it is you go when you die too soon.

His brother and his best friend both spoke
and there was singing—
hymns and "Wind Beneath My Wings" that I doubt Chris would have
    enjoyed—
but there wasn't enough god in me to hum along.

And since I didn't bring any tissues, I wiped my nose on the back
    of my hand
while trying not to be disgusted
at God's conspicuous absence.

It's easy to see Chris's eyes in a stranger's face, even three years past—
easier by far than finding God again in my own reflection

easier by far than finding God in the face of despair.

Anonymous #1, Portsmouth, New Hampshire

FEBRUARY 10

Dear God,
Help us in the days ahead. Help us at school. Take care of the soldiers in
Iraq. Help them in battle and help them on their way home. Save the people
of the world. Amen.

Anonymous #3, Owensville, Missouri

FEBRUARY 11

The Light

The second month of the year
Famed for its fourteenth day
Of lollipops and heart-shaped stickers
Of red roses and boxes of chocolate
Finding comfort in the arms of a loved one
Becomes a challenge and a desperate goal
Rather than the life experience that it was
Meant to be
The comfort we all seek may be
A lot closer than we would have imagined
So close that we may have forgotten
That it has been there the entire time
And will always be there
On the days when we most need comfort
To the days we have been blessed

To forget the loneliness had even existed
Comfort is all around us
In every light
In every smile
In every person

Marcy D. Lombard

FEBRUARY 12

Valentines Day Love!

Chocolate—yummy!
Flowers,
and giving gifts to the people you care for.

It must have been a very strong man
to make a day about love.

Sayre Wilson

FEBRUARY 13

Ode to Jude: patron saint of lost causes

For Jesse

That I could love you any more
Is foolish and silly, verily
To love you deeper than my core
I should laugh a wager to see

Only whole can I be
For I'm half of the charm
But I'm full and complete
When you're in my arms

The epitome of romance
Shines through your soft skin
No more fully could I dance—
When your embrace I am within

Beside and betwixt, my love
Flows like a river of song
Over and under, beneath and above
As wide as forever is long

I love you as much as the sky
Loves the sun, or the sea or the shore
'Tis hopeless, it seems, hard as I try
that my love could ever be more.

Bronny Abbattista

FEBRUARY 14

Prayer for watching my son at 17

Dear God
Help me to keep my heart open
        And my mouth shut

To leave bandages and ointments where they can be found
    but to fight the urge to bang on the door of his cave/room
        when he's huddled there like a wounded bear
            licking his wounds.

To trust that he knows
    that the arms I wrapped around him at two
        are still wrapped around him now—even if he can't see them
        and to trust that You love him now
            no less than you loved me at his age.

The Desert Monks with their vows of silence
    can teach me a lot about being father to my son at 17
Help me to keep my heart open
        And my mouth shut.

Stephen Price

FEBRUARY 15

Dedicated with love to Wil

Holy God, we ask that you bless this prayer with your presence. This prayer comes not only from my heart, but from my girlfriend's heart. Together, we ask for no spectacular miracles in our lives, but that you watch over and protect us. I can only speak for myself when I say how important she is to me and that I hope for you to always grace her days with your presence. However, I know in my soul that she feels the same way. Thus, I dedicate this prayer not to my girlfriend or myself but to the unity we share with one another and with you. May your divine light continue to protect and guide us as well as all couples of this confusing and challenging world, through whatever may come our way. Thank you, Heavenly Father. Amen.

Evan Iwerks

FEBRUARY 16

Bible Study—Samuel

Read 1 Samuel 3:1–10

1) Have you ever had the experience of feeling called or guided to do something, but you could not really identify who or what was calling you so you kept chasing the wrong people?

2) Who is an older mentor in your life who, like Eli, has been able to answer your serious questions and guide you to trust yourself?

3) Do you really (really) believe that God speaks to young people?

PRAYER: God, sometimes it feels like I'm running around yelling, "Here I am," for all the wrong things. I'm eager but I don't have a clue. Help me to "go lie down" and be quiet inside so that I can truly listen to your voice. Amen.

FEBRUARY 17

Single Tear

A
single
tear falls.
a lonely heart
breaks without a
sound. the sun's light
fades, the fire dies out.
yet in this hour, a new flame,
a new fire, a new love, is found.
the sun rises once more, chasing the
night away. the birds sing happily as
the rays of light caress their wings.
and in that minute, a child sees
such beauty as never
before. a tear.

J. S. Price

FEBRUARY 18

I Choose to Love the Light

What does my future hold?
What will happen to me?
Will I ever learn to be bold?
Will I ever truly see?

People and love are all around me,
But will I ever know what they mean?
If I knew it to be true, I could offer so much,
But will I, by myself, ever be really seen?

I'm so confused,
And I'm completely filled with doubt.
I try to ignore the future, which is all a puzzle.
Will this mystery ever be figured out?

New situations can be difficult.

It feels like I'll never adjust,
But then I find the one who was with me all along,
And whom I deeply trust.

These times can be scary.
I find myself often afraid,
But then I remember those who love me,
And by whom I was made.

Will my future be dark,
Or will it be bright?
It can only be what I make of it.
I choose to love the light.

Carlie Cummings

FEBRUARY 19

Declaration

Not in my name
    will you wage war on people I do not know,
    on men, women, and children.
Not in my name
    will you label our country a victim,
    and turn it into an aggressor.
Not in my name
    will you drain my future by creating deficits
    and financial aid for the rich.
Not in my name
    will you steal my children's inheritance
    by drilling and killing and exploiting.
Not in my name
    will you use my money
    to kill.
Not in my name
    will you take my flag, my symbol,
    and soil it with blood.
Not in my name
    will you justify violence
    with arrogance and oil.

Not in my name
   will you claim holy sanction
   to kill God's children.
Not in God's name,
Nor in mine.

Gabriele S. Chase

FEBRUARY 20

Winter

A white blanket covers mother nature,
As she gets her beauty sleep before spring wakes her up.
A gentle wind twirls snowflakes in the air
And rustles the bare trees reaching high into the clear night sky.
Walking on the gravel roads covered in slush
The cold numbs the tip of my nose
Looking up to the stars above
I pray to God:
thank you for the beauty of winter.

Paul Vanderlinde-Abernathy

FEBRUARY 21

See Me For Who I Can Be

For my son, Jesse

Please see me for who I can be
Not what I happen to be acting like at this moment
I didn't do it
It's not my fault
It wasn't my choice
The alcoholic drug-addicted start I was given into this life
By the female who bore me
The woman who did choose to take me in
To love me
Care for me

Raise me
As her own
Sees past all that to who I will be someday
Won't you?

Shelli Valles (adult)

FEBRUARY 22

Society. They have an idea of who we should be. What we should look like. How we should act. They want us to be squeaky clean little angels. They say our opinion matters to them. Then why don't they listen? We are supposed to express ourselves. Share our feelings. Then why is it, if you don't dress like everyone else, you are judged without being given a chance? Don't judge a book by its cover. Isn't that what they are doing by whispering when that person with pink hair walks by? They want us to be good examples to younger people. Look at our examples. They want us to respect our elders no matter what. You give what you get. We are supposed to take responsibility for our actions. We follow what our examples do. They tell us that we should work out our problems using words. Fighting is a last resort. What hypocrites.

Amanda Nickles

FEBRUARY 23

A Prayer for a Yankee Seeking Southern Hospitality

I never connected Mardi Gras and Fat Tuesday
until I was sixteen years old.

Mardi Gras
had always been an excuse for plastic beads,
public drunkenness and the most lewd behavior
you could get away with outside of TV.
It was a southerner's holiday—
a party that was exclusive to New Orleans—
that a New Englander born and bred
could never comprehend.

Fat Tuesday,
on the other hand, that, I could get behind.
It was the day we gorged ourselves on pancakes
for dinner, the day my brother and I got away with pouring
too many chocolate chips in the batter
so we ate a melted goo while our parents were away.
It was delicious and conservative and totally apropos
to our Northeastern upbringing.

That the two should meet,
however, was incomprehensible.
It was segregation we all understood
for the sake of propriety.

It was the difference
in celebrating a sacrifice

we share.

FEBRUARY 24

On Ash Wednesday,
the palms from the previous Easter
are taken and burned.

Holiness and the mundane
blend together to touch each head bent in sacrifice—

humanity is a brushstroke from God's hand.

FEBRUARY 25

Normal

I need to have people around me,
but I'm too independent.
I need you to care for me,
but leave me alone.
I want you to love me,
but I won't change for you.
I hate you so much,
but you're my best friend.

I want to be different,
but not by myself.
I want to know what I want,
but I can't figure it out.
I need to breath,
but I'm suffocating myself.
I want to get out of here,
but I'm just too scared.

I want to cry,
but I won't let myself.
I want to live my life,
but I hide myself away.
I want you to see me,
but from the angle I see myself.
I want to let me be me,
but I don't know if I can . . .

Kimberly Hughes

FEBRUARY 26

The Sims

A while ago, I bought a game called The Sims at the local video game store. For those of you who have not played The Sims, it is a game where you create a family and move them into a house. You can buy things for them and you control every thing they do, such as go to the bathroom and watch television.

A few weeks later, our minister put out a box and allowed anyone to put in any questions they had about religion or God. My question was: Is life like a game of The Sims to God?

After I had asked this question, I thought about it and came up with my own answer: God created everybody, like in The Sims, but God doesn't control everybody. God gave people the power to have their own free will and do what they want to do with their life.

So life to God is partially similar to The Sims, where God creates the family, but does not control what they do. Everyone has the power to make their own decisions and do what they want to.

Ben Merrill

FEBRUARY 27

Reflections on life

To want. A desire, an overflowing wave
searing over the top of rationality.
To see this though presents a burden.
For most, there is conventionality to consider—
engagements, meetings, plans.
This burden continues—to ponder sheer emotions,
Your own, those around you.
What becomes the priority?
Will it be the plan, or
would you venture forth and take this more
attractive interruption?
Do you consider that a choice must be made?
When you choose NOT to choose,
you are submitting to anything—
and find yourself in dire straits.
Consider this:
To be right with yourself
do not sacrifice that for which you strive the most
for a temporary situation.
Appreciate it for what it is, and move on
toward your higher purpose.

Olin Johannessen

FEBRUARY 28

For A Daughter Failing High School Physics
(with apologies to an uncertain Saint Heisenberg)

Dear God,

    If we knew how fast you were going,
                would
        we lose your sense of direction?
    If we knew precisely where
        you were headed, would we speed up
                or slow down?

Thank you, God, that in your quarkiness you leave us
in some dark, preserve
    some
        mystery.
Bless us and keep us

        guessing

J. J. Hunt

FEBRUARY 29

For Our Children, Children of Gay or Lesbian Parents

Defend them, O God, and protect them from their own defenses.

When they are hit by homophobia, may they not feel ashamed inside.
When they are battered by
    the language of oppression,
    the assumptions of heterosexism,
    the fear of difference,
Empower them to stand firm, to celebrate their soul/body/selves.
To relish the freedom of expanding choices, to embrace others who also feel
different.

O God, may they always know
    We mean them no harm, raising them with lesbian parents.
    We mean only love—

Love that nurtures, strengthens, heals, and defies the norm.
Love that loves you, O God.
Love that believes in creation as safe space. Amen.

Leanne Tigert (adult)

ROOM FOR YOUR THOUGHTS

March

MARCH 1

Dear God,
For Lent, I would like to give up selfishness.

When my family needs me, I won't complain—even if the plans I had already made would have been more fun than what I have to do with them. I will not tease my mother when she cries or provoke my father when I can already tell he's in a foul mood. I won't expect my brother to remember to call me back, even if I've left ten messages, and I'll try not to mind when my sister returns my clothes stained. I won't lock my door against the people who love me, even if they've made me so angry that I would be happier alone.

When my friends forget to invite me to a party, I won't sit around and sulk, wishing horrible misfortune on them for their insensitivity. I won't screen my calls—even if there are people I really don't want to talk to because I know they're only going to complain and talk about themselves. I will not spread gossip, even if keeping it a secret makes me want to explode because I know it would be a betrayal of trust and would only hurt my friends and myself. I will not be jealous when I'm not asked out and my best friend is.

For Lent, I will put others first more often, and, instead of resenting it, I'll be happy for them.

God, help me to be strong enough not to give this up through the forty days of Lent and beyond. Amen.

Anonymous, Cambridge, Massachusetts

MARCH 2

Dear Lord,
Please help those who are struggling, for the world in some places can be corrupt. Also, please help those to open their eyes who see past you, so when their time comes they will be ready. I will do my best to help those in need. I just need your help to keep me going strong. In your name, Amen.

Nik Ruff

MARCH 3

Dear God, Sometimes friends are a blessing to us and we give you thanks, but sometimes friends can be hard work and we need your help. Having a friend is like hot chocolate on a cold winter day; thank you, God, for the warmth and comfort of friendship. Having a friend is like working on the same team, toward the same goal; thank you for the companionship and joys of true friends. But sometimes, God, having a friend is like not finding anything good to watch on TV; help us when communication is only one way and we have to set necessary limits. Sometimes having a friend is like your batteries running out on your CD player just when your favorite song comes on; help us, God, when our friends let us down to choose friends wisely and to forgive. Oh, and forgive us, God, when we take our friends for granted, expect too much from them, and become too self-centered in our relationships. We pray this in and through your son Jesus, our friend. Amen.

The Lion's Den, Faith United Church of Christ, Hazelton, Pennsylvania
Dana Kavitski, Katie Zehner, Amber Simone, Amanda Radishofski, Michael Kracum,
Jeff Newburgh, and Rev. Jane Hess

MARCH 4

O Dear Lord,
Please help me. I have done something terrible! My life is falling apart; I need someone to talk to; I think we both know that someone is you. I need forgiveness. I am sorry I disobeyed you. I need help from you. I am very sorry from the bottom of my heart!!! Amen.

Tracy Benson

MARCH 5

Pause for Psalms—Psalm 131

Read Psalm 131.

What is the mood or tone of this psalm? What feelings are expressed? Do you understand the person who wrote this psalm? Can you identify a popular song, movie, or television show in which these emotions are explored? Choose a single verse or line from this psalm and spend some quiet time reflecting on it . . . or simply repeat it over and over again. Create your own words for this psalm. Here is one contemporizing of it.

Psalm 131

Like a weaned child
I quiet myself . . .
a blanket, a thumb,
a poem, a sunset.

I have learned
not to weep and wail,
or whine and whimper.

I am weaned . . .
I can handle life
without hanging on to
the breasts of God.

MARCH 6

Everyone is busy
Not everyone can always join us
I thank God for that one Saturday morning
When twenty-five schedules just worked
I thank God for that birthday

the reason, the excuse I don't need
to see the family I love.

Stephanie Genimatas

MARCH 7

Another Winter Day, God

I'm a bit tempted to just be tired of the cold and the gray and not enough daylight. And yet, winter is not cold everywhere. Some people right now are probably longing for a break from the sun and the heat—missing the beauty of the snow or the magic of a fire gently burning in some cozy living room while it's cold and stormy outside. I'm glad that all four seasons exist, even though I complain more about winter than the other three seasons. Help me to be grateful for all the seasons.

I guess there are gifts that only come in and through the darkness of winter, or maybe by going through the hard parts of winter. So today, remind me of some of these gifts, God. Remind me that I, like the calendar year, have different "seasons" in my life. Remind me, when it seems like tough times are lasting too long, that the spring always comes, and that springs are somehow even more beautiful after a really hard winter. Help me to notice, when I'm tempted to complain about the cold, the beauty of those crystal clear winter nights, when the icy cold sky is full of zillions of stars; remind me that sometimes things get more clear than ever when times are cold and tough and long. And please remind me today of all the ways in which I am given the shelter and warmth and comfort I need to deal with the winter weather. Help me to see your love and caring in the blessings of warm sweaters, working furnaces, hot water, a cup of coffee or tea or hot chocolate, the delicious blessings of hot soup, the extravagant provision of more logs than I need for a fire to burn all evening, the warmth of a good friend's laughter, and the hope and assurance that comes from knowing that no matter how long the winter sometimes seems to drag on, it's a good and necessary time. Things are going on behind the scenes, underneath the surface, and there's nothing I can do but trust these processes and know that spring is always, at worst, not very far away at all. God, there are gifts and blessings to receive and notice during the winter. Help me to see them, and to be truly grateful. Amen.

Bryan Sirchio (adult)

MARCH 8

Dear Heavenly God,
Please let everyone know how much you love them. Please let everyone who is cold and lonely have your heart for warmth and have your words to not be lonely anymore. Please let this prayer we give you come true. Thank you, merciful God. In Jesus' name we pray, Amen.

Kayla Rasmussen

MARCH 9

Rubix Cube

Faith is a difficult thing to tame.

I've always thought it would be like explaining "blue" to a blind person.
There are words and words to shape understanding
but they cannot recreate what has never been experienced.

Faith is sticky but it won't always attach to the right thing.

It seemed to me like giving a child from Somalia a credit card,
then going to a strip mall and expecting understanding
when there has never been a realm of such a reference.

Faith is an ever-evolving beast.

If I took a dog and gave it a cigarette—
taught it how to smoke even—would instinct and alien clash together—
would addiction mean anything in the face of this puzzle?

I cannot capture faith. I cannot paint it or buy it or teach it.
I cannot unravel its secrets.

I can only have it to enjoy.

MARCH 10

I'm walking along, and not looking back,
No idea where I'm going and
I cannot say where I've been.

All I'm asking for is
    Truth
    Love, and
    Hope.
Not true love,
Not an end-all answer.
I'm not asking what they want.
I'm not asking what I need.
Just some calm, peace, serenity.
Not to continue grasping my former lifeline
    which has now fallen dead
I want to be complete,
I want to remember how to dream.
I want to stretch my limitations
    and learn something new.
God, please remind me that no matter
    what I'm looking for
    I can always find it in you.

Nicole Sylvester

MARCH 11

Winter Days

Trees with no leaves—
I like the way you make winter look, Lord.
Trail alone and silent, freshly groomed—
I like the way you make winter sound, Lord.
Pushing up the hill and swooshing down
Technique, technique
rhythm, left, right—
I like the way you make my mind and body remember the moves.
Faster, push, go, go—
I like the way you make my spirit drive harder.
Bail! Cold on the ground
Get up and get going.
You Rule, Lord.

Tom Spencer

MARCH 12

Snow Day

Alarm goes off.
I drag myself out of bed.
It's dark outside, too early to tell.
I go downstairs.
My mom's awake.
She's watching the news for the weather break.
"We had a storm"
She tells me now,
"You have no school."
Yippee! Holy cow!
They list off the schools one by one.
Oh, please, God, no school!
I just wanna have fun!
They say my school.
I jump in the air.
Thanks, God!
but it's only 6 A.M.
I'm awake and that's not fair.

Sayre Wilson

MARCH 13

Birthday

Oh God, we will not be discouraged when we receive a gift that we do not like but we will thank the person who gave us that gift, because it is not the gift that matters—it's the person who gave the gift who matters.

Samantha Benson

MARCH 14

Parent of a Teen Haiku

Instant Messenger—
does not describe family
communication.

I love teenagers.
Also I wear a hair shirt
and enjoy baked crow.

What an argument!
Was that about her hormones,
his independence?

Laundry and dishes—
Why do I sound like a witch?
"I've got the car keys."

Other common disputes . . .
grades, dating, cell phone charges,
one meal together.

"We could be much worse!"
"Trust me . . . what other kids do
is not a comfort."

I'm going online,
then maybe I'll have a chance
to say, "I love you."

MARCH 15

God, thank you for all the things you have given me. You have shown me your love and trust and nothing is greater than that. I know you are always supporting and encouraging me. Even when I do something wrong, you still love me. You are always there, ready to listen and help. Your guidance and, more importantly, your love are unfaltering. Thank you. Amen.

Andrea Nordberg

MARCH 16

Bible Study—Jesus at Twelve in the Temple

Read Luke 2:39–52

1) Have you ever had a complete misunderstanding with your parents in which both sides thought they were right?

2) Can you remember the point when suddenly you wanted adult questions and answers rather than the simpler truths of childhood? Did it shock your family?

3) What's the difference between identifying the same building as "my family's church" and "my Father's house?"

PRAYER: God, there are many markers of adulthood—a paying job, driver's license, voting, personal relationships, selective service. Confirmation, believer's baptism and bar or bat mitzvah are ceremonies of religious maturity. Help me to feel the shift in my relationship with God and others in all contexts. Amen.

MARCH 17

A prayer for the luck of the Irish

Saint Patrick's Day is not a religious event,
unless,
of course,
you're Irish.

Then,
green beer and shamrocks
resemble the cup of Christ and the Trinity . . .
is that sacrilegious or what?

Leprechauns and their pots of gold
speak the truth of apostles—
if only you follow their rainbow
far beyond what you already know.

And get a kiss if you're Irish,
(give a kiss if you're not)
to share the luck and love of one people
throughout a nation of many.

MARCH 18

O God, help me to see
the world beyond my mind.
Help me to know this—
there is more to love
than what the eye can see.
Teach me to overcome the thoughts
that cloud my mind,
and to seek your wisdom
for what you have ahead for me. Amen.

Jeff Ferguson

MARCH 19

A Prayer for Teens in Pain

Dear God,
Please bless those who are in the dark,
They are unable to see,
The wonderful things in life,
You've made for those like me.

They have hatred for their bodies,
Hatred for their lives,
They are drowning in this hatred,
It may even make them die.

They come home and down a bottle of pills,
Or cut their innocent wrists.
They are crying out for help,
As they shake their angry fists.

Scared of who they really are,
Too afraid to change.
But if someone doesn't aid them soon,
It may be too late.

So, God, please let them know you're here,
You can help them see the light.
Because living life is so much fun,
They need a reason to fight.
Amen.

Heather Wehr

MARCH 20

Back before many of us remember, we were touched with water and blessed.

All of our family was present, and the church invited us into its faith.

People offered to bless and keep us safe and to raise us to be the best
people we can be.

The minister asked that God watch over us as with all who ask for God's
guidance and love.

In every church, baptism is different, but the idea remains the same.

Some part of our hearts will forever be touched by the love of our families
and of God.

Mighty is the power of loving and gentle faith in the lives of children.

MARCH 21

Prayer of a Youth Group Leader

Ever-present Creator, source of all that is good, I come before you this
morning rested and refreshed, ready for your will to work through me
today. You have blessed me daily with your presence and your love. You
have surrounded me with a loving, supportive family, with empowering
friends and with young people who are a constant reminder to me of possibility, of passion, and of the beauty of your plan.

Be with me today as I do all of the things that need to be done. Open my
eyes to the needs around me. Open my ears to the still, small voice that I
am sometimes too busy to hear. Open my heart to reach out in patience to
the youth that cross my path today. Bless them as they struggle to discern
your call. Hold their hands to lead them and wrap your loving arms around
them to comfort them, this day, and all of the days of their lives. Amen.

Beverly Ogren (adult)

MARCH 22

Saved by Love

Oh I called out one night,
hope my voice was heard.
I didn't hear the call,
but I knew I would be heard.

Pressed my hands together,
and prayed of my sin.
And you know whose voice I heard singing . . .

Chorus:
You are saved my child,
free from all your sins.
My love will rain down on you,
and cleanse my kin.
And your voice my child, heard from up above,
is saved by love.

I could hold out no doubt,
as I heard those words.
God and his love are saving all the world.
And this peace that I've found,
can be yours too.
Just reach inside and here's what you do . . .

Chorus

And you pray . . . for his love.
Cause all you need is his love.

Chorus

Abigail Reichard

MARCH 23

A Reminder

God reminds me
that I shouldn't stare at myself
in the mirror too much
or too closely

trying to see who I am
because God already knows.

Annie Lalish

MARCH 24

The king has arrived
We lay down palms before him
For his feet are too sacred to touch the unclean ground
He will parade through the city
Glorify the majestic one!
Glorify the majestic one!
Glorify the majestic one!

Greg Kelley

MARCH 25

Under the Same Sky

When you're sad and feeling blue
And no one is there beside you
You must always remember that

Your friends are
Under the same sky,
Looking at the same clouds,
Brightened by the same sun.

When you're stuck in the mud
And all you need is a bud
You must always remember that

Your friends are
Under the same sky,
Looking at the same clouds
Brightened by the same sun.

When all you need is to pray
And get away from a crazy day
You must always remember that

You are always
Under the same sky,
Looking at the same clouds,
Brightened by the sun.

God made the sky,
And the clouds,
And shines the sun, created
To hold love for everyone.

God is always just a prayer away.

Carly Lagasse

MARCH 26

Angel

I saw an angel this morning,
I took it by the hand.
I sprouted wings,
And there was a halo atop my head.
I was about to enter a better world,
Of love and laughter—
No madness or grief.
I saw an angel this morning . . .

Johanna Bozuwa

MARCH 27

The Key

The key to life
unlock the doors
of the soul
and spirits forever soar
for the key to living
the key to life
to find the love
the love of your life

Crystal Sipe

MARCH 28

Prayer of a High School Girls Basketball Coach and Physical Education Teacher

My prayer is an individual one—I don't say it with the team, but it is for both of the teams playing, my family, and myself. I say this prayer before every game that I coach and most games that I am a fan at for I will never forget the opportunities that I have been blessed with in this life. On this particular night, my daughter was playing at Tufts University, and her grandfather, who had played many years before, would be watching from heaven. I had another game so I sent the words to her.

The Anthem Prayer, from Mom to Kristin:

I figure that the national anthem will be playing at the same time in my gym as at your game, so as I always do at "rocket's red glare" I will close my eyes and pray for a competitive game with good sportsmanship, free from injury to all players . . . then I always ask God to bless my two honeys (my children) even when they're with me, but especially when they are not. And bless my husband/best friend. Then I always remember to thank God for letting me be born in this country to the families I was born into and married into, and for all the opportunities God has given me in this life, especially to be a mother, a teacher, and a coach.

Jane Heil

MARCH 29

A bird, over the highway—
too big to be a hawk.
Its body brown as one,
but its tail, spread fan, white,
and its head, too . . .
only the second eagle I have ever seen.

Emilie Karr

MARCH 30

Passover

One week without bread is like a summer without ice cream
One week without pasta is like an autumn without colors
One week without corn syrup is like a winter without hot chocolate—
     or snow
One week without leavening is nothing compared to the forty years my
     ancestors spent wandering a desert to find their holy land.

Sarah Fineberg-Lombardi

MARCH 31

Prayer from a Coach for Creative Problem-Solving Programs

God, please help these children to recognize their special talents and see
how to use them to serve this team as well as the communities that they
represent. Help them discover their creativity and learn to use it to solve the
problems they face with each other now as well as the problems they will
face in their lives in the future.

Help them to bring their individual skills and ideas together to work as a
team, and to recognize the advantages of coming together and sharing ef-
forts to solve the problems of the world.

Help me develop in them the abilities and values that will enable them to
make our world a better, more prayerful place to live and work and play.
Amen.

Diane Karr

ROOM FOR YOUR THOUGHTS

April

APRIL 1

I Fear Not the Wrath of April

I fear not the wrath of April
Although the arachnids rise from their winter chambers and approach me with
menacingly jointed legs
I fear not the wrath of April
Although territorial cat fights wake me at 3:00 A.M.
I fear not the wrath of April
Although the fisher cat once again pierces the night with its morbid cry
I fear not the wrath of April
Although the pollen makes my nose dysfunctional
And I feel the stingers of 137 wasps in my eyes
I fear not the wrath of April
For the snow has melted
Another season that the Lord created has arrived
The fields are now green and ripe for frolicking

Greg Kelley

APRIL 2

God,
I saw you today in a puppy's eyes. I heard you today in a baby's cries.
I touch the air and I feel you there.
The sun, the sky, the earth, the trees. Sandy beaches and autumn breeze.
Spring, summer, winter, fall. It's amazing how you made it all.
You created life; it's not a game. How you can heal the sick and cure the pain.
Be with the children without a home. Lifeless adults, faces wind-blown.
You are the laughter. You are the light. You are the scared throughout
    the night.
Millions of prayers everyday. Cries of help in every way.
Be with all of us from here on and out. Every country here and about.

Jessica Messina

APRIL 3

If God
(or Darwin)
created the world in seven days
(a billion years)—
who do I blame for Daylight Savings Time?

If God,
I can forgive you
because seven days doesn't allow much time for detail;
but what happened with that ineffable plan?

If Darwin,
I can question you
because holes still exist in scientific theory;
but shouldn't someone have been researching this?

If neither faith nor science are willing to help,
to whom can I go if I want to reclaim that lost hour
of sleep unceremoniously stolen from me at 2 A.M.
in the spring of every year?

APRIL 4

O dear loving God,
Thank you for letting us have peace in the world. Help the people in the nursing home, Emmaus Home, and the foster kids who are looking for parents. Thank you for taking time to hear my prayers. Amen.

Woody Schlottach

APRIL 5

Pause for Psalms—Psalm 104

Read Psalm 104.

What is the mood or tone of this psalm? What feelings are expressed? Do you understand the person who wrote this psalm? Can you identify a popular song, movie, or television show in which these emotions are explored? Choose a single verse or line from this psalm and spend some quiet time reflecting on it . . . or simply repeat it over and over again. Create your own words for this psalm. Here is one contemporizing of it.

Psalm 104

God, in a chemise of sunlight,
you pull aside the curtain of the dawn,
and you step on the
floorboard of the ocean,
walk down the wind's street,
catch the greyhound of the clouds.

God, you work construction,
laying all foundations,
paving the cement of the deep.
You are electrician of waterfalls,
plumber of springs,
Paul Bunyan with the thunder.

God, old zookeeper, you
care for wild asses, goats, cud-eater cattle,
an aviary of bright birds,
a lion's den and—strangest of all,

stranger than shark tank, dolphin show—
your human animal.

God, you are moon mathematician,
plowboy of earth,
sailor with crinkled eyes,
tender of beasts, demolition expert,
life-guard . . . blowing mouth to mouth
breath into all creatures.

APRIL 6

Dearest Lord,
Give me the strength and power to overcome myself. Give me the strength
to believe in myself and not care about what others say. Give me the power
to be the best I can be at all times. In your name I pray, Amen.

C. J. Garza

APRIL 7

Prayer of a Pastor

God, this baby I held in my arms and baptized into our local church and all
of God's Church is now asking adult questions about the literal truth of the
Bible stories and the hypocrisy of congregational decisions. Yesterday's infant
is challenging me about caring for the poor, feeding the homeless, opening
our doors to people of all orientations, protesting government policy.

Help! Help preaching from my pulpit to be both young and grown up
enough to be Good News for every generation. At least, God, keep me listening! Amen.

APRIL 8

Jesus Saves the Day

Dear Lord, we thank you for your only son
Jesus, you have made our sins disappear
Thinking of Heaven we can only imagine the fun

Thinking of death we need not fear
For in April we recall the time you were crucified
Now you have saved us from your father's wrath
So many will live who would have died
You have washed away our sins and cleared us a path

Greg Kelley

APRIL 9

Somewhere up there
in the mysteries of the Milky Way,
You're watching me and
I know that you're there.
You catch me when I fall,
and lift me up again.
You care about me and
shine a light on the path of righteousness to guide me.
You teach me about good and evil and
forgive me when I'm wrong.
But most of all, you love me.
Thank you, dear God. I will always love you.
Amen.

Meredith Grubb

APRIL 10

Forty long nights

Lent is no meat
to the Catholics,
except for Friday
when fish finds its way to the feast.

Lent is no chocolate
to my mother,
except for Sunday
when even a minister deserves respite from abstention.

Lent is no problem
to me,
every day an exception
for promises I don't keep.

Lent is too much a New Year's resolution—
promise of sacrifice rarely delivered.

Lent is forgotten celebration
to us,
the strength sacrifice supplies
a wilderness unknown.

APRIL 11

Salvation

It was 2:00 A.M. back in April 1994
Randolph had in mind a corrupt task
He crept from house to house, searching for an unlocked door
No one would ever recognize him with his brand new ski mask.
Soon a doorknob turned and he stepped inside
A silhouette emerged from the shadows and yelled, "Hey!"
Randolph knew it was too late but still tried to hide
The resident turned on the light and it was as bright as day
Randolph unexpectedly looked into the eyes of his old high school buddy Fred
He removed his mask and cried, "I'm terribly sorry! What can I do?"
Fred answered, "Repent to the Lord and you won't end up dead."
Jesus saved Randolph and he will save you!

Greg Kelley

APRIL 12

Rejoice in the Sun's rise
and laugh with the Rain's fall

Practice compassion and patience
and respect the Power of Peace

Whitney Peterson

APRIL 13

Morning Blessing—Waking Up Our Body Parts

Bless our Eyes, may they help us to always see your beautiful gifts all around us.
Bless our Ears, may they hear the word of God every day.
Bless our Mouth, may it speak kind words and tell about acts of love.
Bless our Brain, may it hold all the knowledge it can,
    may it always remember music, may it hold the memory of God forever.
Bless our Heart, may it keep God in it forever, helping us love one another.
Bless our Back, may it structure our body forever so we go straight and true
    to God.
Bless our Hands, may they allow us to communicate
    through our writing to others,
    through our praying to God, and through sign language for those who
        cannot hear.
Bless our Feet, may they let us walk the woods and keep ourselves healthy
    so we can do the work of God.
        Every day the sun rises. Each person moves every joint in the body.
        Every day we give ourselves to you. Amen.

Youth Fellowship-Confirmation Group, Machias, Maine

APRIL 14

Reflection of a Commissioned Minister in Christian Education

Recently, I ran across a Jell-O mold in an antique shop that gave me one of
those moments of "flash back" to my childhood. It was a mold like one
that my mom used to make Jell-O in. Yes, she would do that, every once in
awhile, just because. There wasn't usually a particular reason why. It just
made a family meal a little extra special!

Anyway, those memories caused me to ponder. I began thinking about
my own children, and all of the kids I work with at church and in the community. What am I doing that's making them feel extra special? What am I
doing to create memories for them? I'm part of a "molding" process that
goes WAY beyond gelatin.

My prayer? The words are in the hymn . . . "Spirit of the living God,
fall afresh on me. Melt me, mold me, fill me, use me. Spirit of the living
God, fall afresh on me." Amen.

Lynn Butterbrodt

APRIL 15

Sisters for Life

She'd scream at me
I'd yell right back
Someone got angry,
And then they'd attack.

We tried to comfort
And help each other
We sort of had to
On account of our mother

Some years went by
Now we're always at the mall
We share our music
And I watch her pitch a softball

We still fight sometimes
But when one has to cry
We're there for each other
My sister and I

Our mother's words have stuck with us
"Some day you'll leave to be some handsome man's wife
Don't let the fights get too big
You're sisters for life.

Jaclyn Kregling

APRIL 16

Bible Study—Joseph

Read Genesis 37:2–8, 12–24

1) Do you know of family situations of people from school or church where one child is obviously favored by the parents over the other children? What are the effects of this on everyone in the family?

2) How would you have felt about Joseph if he told you his dream?

3) Why did Joseph's brothers throw him in the pit (and subsequently send him to Egypt)? Why is violence never justified?

PRAYER: God, I confess the deep human feeling that sometimes I would like to "kill" somebody in my family, but I know that, if I gave in to that violence, it would destroy me. Help me in my personal family situation to seriously consider the feelings of every family member. Amen.

APRIL 17

This bullet meant for you

On Good Friday I imagine the sky turned black
and the clouds rolled in tinged with gold.
The grass pressed flat to the earth,
although the wind was stilled
and quiet. Shutters banged
against empty windows and the gates would swing
back and forth on oiled hinges,
moved by an indefinable fear
of standing still.

Around the cross,
a murderous murmur would rise
and fall, a pretty cadence
to keep Jesus company.
This was entertainment—
one more criminal punished in the way of the world
was nothing to take notice of.

And not many people would have asked,
"my God, my God—
why have you forsaken me?"

because, you see,
God's death was nothing out of the ordinary.

Maria I. Tirabassi

APRIL 18

God,
I saw you today in many others. You reminded me of how you began this world with Adam and Eve and now your success leads to billions more people. It reminds me of how proud you must be of your creation of humanity.

Nick, Melrose, Massachusetts

APRIL 19

I won't be a stranger in my own life. I love my family. I love my friends.
I have every chance to share this.
If today was the only day, I'd have lived it.
If tomorrow was the last, there's not a moment I'd regret.

There is a bird on my shoulder who tells me "now is the time to fly."

If I don't reach a goal, it wasn't set in the first place.
If I make it to the top of the hill and see the next horizon, I'll keep walking.
If I make it to the cliffs, I'll get a running start,
spread my arms abreast a brazen wingspan
and take a swan dive.

Anonymous, Ojai, California

APRIL 20

A Prayer for Three Sons

God of all creation,
    Creator of male and female.
You have given us the gift of three sons,
    born out of love, born to make a difference in this world.
Thank you that they were each uniquely created,
    forged into men with courage, compassion, and energy.
How we have prayed them through geometry, broken hearts, and bad habits,
    how we despaired when they succumbed and sold themselves short.

Be with our young men, oh God,
    energize them with your confidence.
        Instill in them a knowledge that they have a purpose here on earth
        to serve you and others.
            Assure them that you have equipped them with the gifts
            and personality to face all that will come into their world.

For I declare my great love for these young heroes,
    young boys I cared for with my time and energy
    young men carrying my dreams and hopes.
Help me to let them go.
    Guide me to accept the choices they make
        as I entrust them into your forgiveness and grace
        so they will be fortified by their relationship with you
        and fulfilled in the potential you have created in them.
I pray this out of my love for them and my faith in you.
Amen.

Gayle Murphy (adult)

APRIL 21

Losing

I was worried about separation
Losing the ideals I had held onto for so long
Because we were definitely spreading apart
and I knew that
I knew that nothing would ever be the same again
but if we lose some
and gain some along the way
I know I'll end up all right
because what's the point of hanging onto something
that makes you miserable

Kimberly Hughes

APRIL 22

Prayer for Wholeness

O, Creator,
    Loving Light and Power,
what world have we made ourselves
    to live in?
Broken families, broken homes,
Broken promises, broken hearts,
Broken windows, broken bones,
Broken light broken by broken trees.
    Lift us up, God,
each one of us a broken child
    with broken dreams,
and into our broken bodies
    breathe.
Heal us with your moving Spirit,
private music and silent words
whispered softly to the heart.

Gabriele S. Chase

APRIL 23

Early one morning, the women went to Jesus' grave.

All they found was an empty tomb, but then Jesus appeared to them to say
    he was risen.

Scared, they ran to find the disciples and share this astonishing news.

Together, Jesus' friends saw their risen savior and spoke with him.

Even though they were a little afraid, they were also amazed and excited.

Returning to earth and his people, Jesus shared his life anew.

APRIL 24

God
The happiness in hearts
The beauty of love
The strength and compassion of a friend
The knowledge and education in youth, and the interest to learn
The respect for others

God
The breeze in the air
The wind through the trees
The colors of nature
The four seasons
The green, green grass beneath our feet
The sun in the sky to brighten our days

God is pure love and happiness

Carly Lagasse

APRIL 25

I don't know if I still believe in the Easter bunny,
rising early to search out little plastic gift eggs,
standing in deep sunrise fog
singing "holy holy holy."

I don't know if I still believe in holy holy holy,
raising my voice over early spring roar,
reading scripture to the birds
praising God, Christ, and the Holy Spirit.

I don't know if I still believe in God, Christ, and the Holy Spirit,
shifting my weight foot to foot,
recalling the cross
hoping to rediscover God, Christ, and the Holy Spirit as the holiest
    of Easter gifts.

APRIL 26

Easter

Easter is here! Birds are singing and special church ceremonies are filling the air. Grandmothers are knitting and children are playing. The air is fresh from the spring flowers and everything is perfect. Thank you, God, for this special Easter Day. Amen.

Sanne Brown

APRIL 27

The Calling Place

Silence nestles deep in the woods
Entrenched in my every breath
Everything is hazy
And the trees loom in front of me
Like giants
The air is thick with a
Misty, morning fog
And my outstretched hand seems to
Fade away in front of my face
Each step I take
Uncertain
yet somehow steady
Crunching in the earth
Leading me to the
Blurred horizon of my fate
The sights behind me grow undefined
While the path in front of me
Becomes clear
Strength surges through the ground beneath my feet
a force that knows all,
there is peace,
And stillness
That can be found in no other place
A wind comes up to lick my cheek
One cheek among the many timeless faces
Birds call out longingly from the trees in a chorus

Echoed by the caw of a
Solitary crow
Only the wisdom of the wind can tell
Where I will end up.
What adventure lies ahead
Time slows
And settles into everything it touches
Time is like a cloud of history and life here
Clinging to almost forgotten memories
Like one who has lost a friend
This is the place I am bound to
No one can live in this world
Yet it is somehow the one I understand
It is here that one is surrounded by mystery
Here where all life combines into one breath
here that one is consumed
by the unity of home
Here
In the calling place

Lauren Hoelle

APRIL 28

Litany for Transgender Issues

For all your children who are not at home in their own bodies,
who know you made them the other gender,
we pray to the God of new birth.

God, hear our prayer.

For families struggling with the issues of gender transition
and caring for all their members,
we pray to the God of reconciliation.

God, hear our prayer.

For youth groups reaching out to gender minorities,
for youth leaders and campus ministers responding to
frightening recognitions and fragile relationships,
we pray to the God of compassion.

God, hear our prayer.

For churches who are seeking to open their hearts to all your children,
whether gay, lesbian, transgender, or bisexual,
and for their balanced loving process,
we pray to the God of justice and of peace.

God, hear our prayer.

Anonymous (adult)

APRIL 29

Our heavenly Father,
We live in a go-go world. Sometimes I feel like children get lost in the mix. I
want to give thanks to the adults in the world that take that extra minute to
connect with children. I don't feel like there are enough adults that can do
that. Those adults are very special to the world. Help me to be one. Amen.

Jason Miller

APRIL 30

Hand in Hand

Come take me by the hand,
I want a lifelong friendship,
My friend.
I want to live life hand in hand,
Don't let me down, my friend.
I will be there for you
Wherever you are.
I will never lose sight of you,
I hope you do not lose sight of me.
Let me take you hand in hand,
My friend,
Hand in hand.

Johanna Bozuwa

ROOM FOR YOUR THOUGHTS

May

MAY 1

Shades

pull the shades away
live another day
pull the shades away
live the life of sun
pull the shades away
see the twinkling stars in the distance
they will give you hope to live on
live your life to its fullest

Johanna M. Bozuwa

MAY 2

Dear God,
Spring is approaching and the flowers are blooming. The deadness is gone and laughter is in the air. I thank you for spring.

Taylor Renaud

MAY 3

Dear God,
We thank you for the gift of Mother's Day. Mothers are a blessing bestowed upon us in this imperfect world. They are here to give us a taste of your love on earth and provide your spirit in times of sadness and trouble. Hear our thanks today, for the happiness they bring to our lives. We also remember those who are hurting today, O God. Those who have lost a child and those who have lost a mother. We ask you to surround them with your love, help heal the empty space. Remind them of wonderful memories created. Bless also the women of our world who are filling the role of mother. Help them to see their important role. Provide them with support; encourage them to seek out new opportunities to be part of this beautiful gift. Thank you, God, for the loving way in which you mother us.

Katherine M. Spain

MAY 4

Thank You, Mom

Thank you, Mom,
For all that you have done
For carrying me for nine months,
And then for putting up with me for 18 years more.
Thank you, Mom
For so kindly showing that you were right.
Thank you, Mom,
For all that you provided—
From the soccer and basketball games,
to the dreaded parent-teacher conferences, PTSA meetings.
Thank you, Mom,

For guiding me back home
when I was "lost."
And then for making sure I didn't get "lost" again.
Thank you, Mom,
for staying up late,
when I was weak or sick.
Never leaving for more than five minutes at a time.
Thank you, Mom,
For considering the situations that we have been through,
When we both knew what you could have done,
Instead of agreeing and listening.
Thank you, Mom,
for the sound advice,
that I have yet to use.
To go further than what is expected.
Thank you, Mom,
For encouraging me
to follow my hopes, dreams, heart, and faith
and telling me not to listen to what others say about me.
Thank you, Mom,
For all that I didn't mention,
'Cause, if I did,
Then this poem would never end.
Thank you, Mom,
for that is all I really need to say.

Dave Adkins

MAY 5

Pause for Psalms—Psalm 134

Read Psalm 134.

What is the mood or tone of this psalm? What feelings are expressed? Do you understand the person who wrote this psalm? Can you identify a popular song, movie, or television show in which these emotions are explored? Choose a single verse or line from this psalm and spend some quiet time reflecting on it . . . or simply repeat it over and over again. Create your own words for this psalm. Here is one contemporizing of it.

Psalm 134

Nightwatchers—praise God.

Owl, skunk, raccoon,
cat and wild cat,
nurse and police officer,

trucker, all-hour-diner staff,
poet, third-shift worker,
lonely walker, waiter, wanderer,

stars and moon,
wind over the hills,

Nightwatchers—praise God.

MAY 6

God bless the troubled kids who go to parties and get drunk and wild
   almost every night.
God bless kids who are abused or don't have a good home life.
God bless the kids who don't think they care about life anymore and try
   to kill themselves.
God bless the kids who are so addicted to drugs that they have to keep
   having them and having them.
God bless the kids who are alcoholics and help them resist the urge to
   take a drink.
And God bless all of us who are friends or just classmates of kids with
   these problems so we can have the courage to say something, to reach
   out and help. It's hard but you can make it easier. Amen.

Ben Merrill

MAY 7

Prayer of an Alcoholic

Dear God, Higher Power, Light in the Darkness,
I have taken my own twelve steps. Now I put my "anonymous" in the
offering plate so that I can mentor all these young people who are hooked

on booze or drugs, sex, shopping, even the Internet. I know about addiction. I've got the years of ashes to show for it. Help me trim the "dimly burning wicks" of the kids in my church and outside of it. It's not going to be easy. They will make me mad. I won't be the right person for some of them. Some of them will cling too tightly, will flatter me with their dependence. I promise to let go. I promise to be a safe sponsor. I promise to turn the healing over to you. Bless me in my intention and bless these young men and women who are going to be candles in their own generation. Amen.

Anonymous (adult)

MAY 8

Nature

Your eyes are the sky,
Your hair the leaves,
Your body the Earth,
Whenever I look outside, dear God,
I see you. Amen.

Stefan Triana

MAY 9

Statement of Faith

When I think of Jesus I think of the person who died on the cross for my sins. He is my one and only true God and Savior. When I accepted God into my life it was the best moment of my life. I was at church camp last year and Katie Cooper, my brother Zach, and another camp counselor had a long talk with me. Katie said a prayer and I repeated after her. During that prayer I felt like the Holy Spirit just went through me. After the prayer we stood there and just hugged for a while. From that moment on my life got a lot simpler. Things in life just seemed to fit. My life was changed.

I look at things with a new perspective. Like whenever something bad happens I don't get mad and angry like I used to because it was supposed to happen that way and something good will come out of it when God thinks that I am ready for it. I think that God gives us only what we can handle. Sometimes in life things can get so bad that we question God. But God doesn't give us bad things in life. Just at these worst moments of our life, we can draw ourselves closer to God and build up the relationship.

I believe that God has our lives already planned out for us; we just have to make the right choices and go down the right paths. And if we go off the path God is there to lead us again where we need to go.

I believe that Jesus died for our sins on the cross and that he rose again.

I think that the sky is like a giant snow globe and we are inside as God is on the outside looking down at us.

I believe that there is a heaven and that when you die that there are gates to heaven with God there waiting to guide you where you need to go.

I believe that if you accept Jesus as your savior and you follow his ways, you will go to heaven.

I think of my life as a race to the finish line. We were put on this earth to do a mission to make the world better. But once we finish our mission then we go home with God. A lot of people think that people who don't go to church and say that they are Christians really aren't. But some of the strongest Christians have their own worship time with God and are really close. I don't think that just going to church is enough to get a strong solid relationship with God because you get more with a one-on-one with God.

So we ask ourselves, why is church so important? Going to church puts you in the company of other Christians, you can become spiritually uplifted through a song or a sermon, and all in all it keeps you on the right path.

Meghan Krato

MAY 10

Spring

Flowers blowing in the wind at last
Grass, reborn and soft again
The sun shining more brightly than any other time
Trees' new budding leaves are ruffled by a small breeze

The renaissance of the year
The cold, hard winter is gone
Everything is new
Spring is everywhere.

Johanna Bozuwa

MAY 11

First date hallelujah

Her:
Is my hair all right?
Does he like my shoes?
Where are we going?
Does he know I don't eat carbs?
How long did he spend getting ready?
Does he like my dad?
What is that smell—the upholstery?
Does my dad like him?
Will he kiss me soon?
Does my breath smell?

Him:
Should I hold her hand?
Does she like to dance?
Is my deodorant working?
Does she eat Mexican?
When will she kiss me?
Does her dad like me?
Was that a rotteweiler I saw in her backyard?
Does she know I'm a virgin?
How long can I keep talking about the weather?
Does she like me?

God:
Why did I make everybody so insecure?

MAY 12

There for Me (a song)

I was walking alone, feeling confused.
Feeling left out, put down and used.
I needed a friend whom I could talk to . . .
So I closed my eyes, and I turned to you.

You were there for me, you were there for me . . .
Now I know that you'll always be, there for me.

Through both good and bad, you've been by my side.
You let me know things will be all right.
When I've been lost, you've helped me find my way.
You've given me strength, you've given me faith.

'Cause you were there for me, you were there for me . . .
Now I know that you'll always be, there for me.

I'll have more battles that I'll have to face,
But I'll turn to you each of those days.
And I know I will find a friend in you,
I will follow you like I've promised to . . .

And when I'm walking alone, feeling confused,
Feeling left out, put down or used . . .
When I need a friend, I know just what I'll do . . .
I'll close my eyes and I'll turn to you.

You'll be there for me, you'll be there for me,
Now I know that you'll always be, there for me.

Emma Catlett-Sirchio

MAY 13

Mother-God, you hold us in your arms with so much tenderness, so much love. You felt us inside of you before we were born. Then you helped us walk when our steps were shaky and understood our babbling, which we wanted to be language. You were flexible to our rebellions, supportive of our gifts, dependable with your discipline, understanding of all our troubles. Mother-God, we trust the universe, even the most frightening things that may happen, because of your faithful presence. Amen.

Anonymous, Des Moines, Iowa

MAY 14

The Blessings of Teaching in a Small Town

One of my gifts from teaching a fair number of years in the community where I also live is watching the flow of the seasons. Not only are my seasons measured as fall turns to winter and then to spring, but as freshmen become sophomores then juniors and eventually graduate. I receive a new group each autumn and say good-bye to them in spring. For a brief period of time from August through June, I get to teach them my subject, help them with their fears, share their victories, give them my spin on the world outside, and listen to theirs. Sometimes we click and sometimes we don't. I can never really know the world they live in, but I can try to give them some insights into the ones in which I have lived. Joy has come in meetings years later at county fairs and hardware stores when I get to hear their stories of the lives they have created since high school and realize I had a small part in their lives.

Robert Young (chemistry teacher)

MAY 15

If Job wore glitterpaint I could pray to him

God, I went to prom in blue tulle sparkles
accompanied by a gay boy
whose hair matched my princess-pouf splendor.
We danced to Tyler's piano jazz
under a chilled May moon
and there were no thoughts of romance.
We didn't kiss or toast to love
or sex
and I didn't feel like I was missing out
on a cultural rite of passage.

No, I didn't regret a minute of the dance,
of glitter-painted eyes and of upswept hair—
in fact, I was glad he hadn't already made plans
since I had been turned down
seven times
before I heard him remark that I looked
lovelier than a garden in full bloom.

God, I went to prom in blue tulle sparkles
accompanied by a gay boy
who has suffered since that night
under a chilled May moon
because his idea of romance
isn't considered a cultural right of passage.
He misses out on kisses and toasts
and sex,
lovelier than a garden in full bloom,
and nobody asks him to dance.

MAY 16

Bible Study—David

Read 1 Samuel 16:1, 4–13

1) In what different ways and places are people judged by external appearance? Has that ever happened to you?

2) David was the unexpected choice of Samuel. Have you ever been chosen for something when neither you nor anyone else expected it?

3) David was anointed to be king when he was a teenager. The reality did not happen until many years later. Do you have potential in you that can only mature after many years, experiences, and education? What are they?

PRAYER: God, help us not to judge by "tall and old" but by the heart. Guide us to experience our own anointing of spirit for tasks that are beyond us now, and keep us attentive to the hidden gifts of others. Amen.

MAY 17

A Mother's Gift

Dear God,
You can be one person in this world, but you can also mean the world to one person. It takes passion and drive to achieve this, but you must believe in both yourself and the person. My mother gave me life and I am eternally grateful to her. In my heart I strongly feel that she needs a prayer. She does

not need a prayer for success or happiness because she is an amazing person who mesmerizes me every day of my life. Prayer is not always for forgiveness or to ask for something but it is also for thankfulness. I am ever so grateful for my mother. Her beauty both inside and out shines through to the world every second of the day. It is a sincere privilege to me to be born to such an extraordinary human being. Her love, care, and immense heart are reflected through the people she has touched and through myself as well. "You are remembered in this world not because of what you do, but by what you do for other people." If I remember anything she ever told me, please, God, let it be this. Let me lead my life to the extreme greatness that she has. True love is not only between a husband and wife, but also between a mother and daughter. Dear God, I truly hope she knows how I feel about her. She is my world, my everything. What I wouldn't give for her to spend a day in my shoes and realize how much she means to me. She needs not a prayer of help, but only a prayer of love, blessing, and gratitude. My Lord, please help me to make it evident to my mother how much I care. I thank you for listening and may you also feel her ray of light, beauty, and love.

Beth Harlow

MAY 18

Sanity

Exemption
might as well be synonymous with
Freak.
No, I'm not taking my finals.
Last year I only took two.
Two.
Out of six.
But taking any you don't have to equals
Insanity.
Well, I guess I'm a nut then,
no child prodigy,
no genius.
So sorry if that offends you . . .
Not.
But if one more person says the word

Valedictorian
I'll snap.
I really will.
then I can happily go on earning A's,
but from inside the Loony bin.

Gabriele S. Chase

MAY 19

"As Jesus was saying these things, a woman in the crowd called out,
'Blessed is the mother who gave you birth and nursed you.'" (Luke 11:27)

Mothers are there . . .

Mothers are there to care for you,
Mothers are there to see you through.
Mothers are there to pick you up when you're down,
Mothers are there to kiss away your frown.

Mothers are sent from heaven above,
to care for you and show you love.
Mothers are angels, who guide you through,
and help you make right decisions in all you do.

And on this day we take time to celebrate
the mothers in our lives we love and appreciate.
Mothers, grandmothers, aunts, and Christian women, too,
Thank you for leading us and guiding us in all we do,
The Youth of Providence Church want to say, "We love you."

Tory Myers (Providence Church, Chesapeake, Virginia)

MAY 20

Dear heavenly Father, Please be with the families of soldiers in Iraq. Let the
soldiers come home safe with no injuries. Thank you for everything you
will do for us in the time to come. In Jesus' name we pray. Amen.

Anonymous #1, Owensville, Missouri

MAY 21

Prayer of a Parent in a Time of War

God, I think about my own teenager and teenagers around the world. War has shrunk the globe and I see myself as every scared parent, every proud parent, every guilty parent who has been too busy "making a living" to shape a safe life for the next generation.

I pray for young people in military service and protest marches. I pray for new voters and young people who decide to become politicians. I pray for peace-making and justice-making and hope-making and I pray for young people to become peacemakers, justicemakers, hopemakers.

I pray for all of these and for their children . . . both the ones who will call me "Gran" and the ones all across the world whom I may never see, but who may live because of my choices and my encouragement of today's teenagers to choose. Amen.

MAY 22

It's now the end of a successful spring.
Now songs of summer, we begin to sing.

I think of both the end, of school and of peers
and also the beginning, of college and careers.

Graduation is approaching, and whatever will I do?
My choices are endless, but your word will guide me through.

Perhaps I'll join the forces, fighting for the freedoms we relish
Working for Americans everywhere and learning to be unselfish.

If it should turn out that the military's not for me,
I'd still work hard, and remember how this country came to be.

I'll honor and support them, and uphold my American pride
And I'll remember forever what Memorial Day should signify.

But first I ask your wisdom, to help me in the present day.
Make me wise and stronger so that I can live your way.

The future may be indecisive, but one thing is for sure,
You will be there beside me, wherever I may go.

Jeff Ferguson

MAY 23

My confirmation,
I was nervous but not scared.
God helped me through it.

For my friend, sadly,
it was not an easy choice
and she had regrets.

Her parents were strict,
wanted her to go through with it.
It was hard for her.

I've wondered since then
whether it made any sense to God—
turning faith to fear.

Anonymous, Boston, Massachusetts

MAY 24

Awakening, the day unfolds around you.
Sleeping fast, then coming upward,
toward the place of consciousness.

Now taking in the light all around you,
looking at objects, instances, people—
CONTEXTS of your very life.

Open yourself up, and see all that
you can be should you start anew.

Use that light—add a sense of simplicity.
Gain a new perspective on why we are all here.

Find a love—and hold fast until
you've enraptured yourself completely;
becoming all that you love in

another person—enjoying that feeling,
and showing your love to that love in return.
Seeing all newness and wonder,
lighting up, moving forward,
wanting to prove your higher power.

Seek up, go forth,
and put your mark on the earth.

Olin Johannessen

MAY 25

Dear God,
Thanks for making spring. It feels good to hit a homerun. It's a great feeling at home after the umpire calls you safe.

Chris Brown

MAY 26

A Graduation Prayer

Dear Jesus, thank you for carrying me through these past years of school and allowing me to graduate. Please be with me and my peers as we move on to our next stage of life. Help us carry out your will and to remain in your light. Help us to make the decisions that will make you proud of us. Give us courage, Savior, to not be afraid and to be able to complete the next task you set in front of us. Keep us always safe, caring and honoring. In your holy name, I pray. Amen.

Jaclyn Kernander

MAY 27

Prayer

In the coming hours and days, please help me to have the courage, the strength, and the grace to rise up and face the tasks and ordeals that will surely confront me in my life. Help me to be steadfast in faith and in deed so that I may stay the course of action and finish stronger than I ever thought I could. And, by your grace, allow me to gain from my experiences so I may accomplish more in the future. Amen.

Michael Smith

MAY 28

A movie theatre manager's prayer

God, see them flashing through life at twelve frames per second. God, take them off the screen. Grow them into dimensions that cannot be captured in any medium. Make them more than an image, more than a model, more than a byte of sound. Blow each of them up into the only image, the holy image, the image in which each was created. Direct them according to your script, your Word, your Love. Amen.

Dianne Prichard (adult)

MAY 29

Here are some juicy thoughts on the month of May:

For me, May is the month of music. The school year is ending. All the year's practice and hard work comes together with the last few concerts of the school year and it is in that month that I am the happiest. Going from one audience to another, each time going onto the stage tense and my mind full of music, and coming off feeling satisfaction cover me like a warm blanket. And theatre practicing, always lots of practicing, then a concert, then more practicing for another concert. I love this month, sharing what I think of as my gift with everyone else. The month ends and I feel like I have just run a very long race and won it.

Ben Levergood

MAY 30

It is very important to pray. You should pray for your loved ones in sickness and in health. Also pray for anyone whether it's a poor guy or rich guy. Pray for peace and forgiveness. Pray to God to thank him if something good happens. That is what you should pray for.

Kaleigh DiPietro

MAY 31

A prayer for procrastinators:

Please, God, can we talk later?

Matthew Karr

ROOM FOR YOUR THOUGHTS

June

JUNE 1

I can look backwards from the tip of a twig and see the entire tree, the network of changes that led up to that tiny point. From the trunk, to the branches, to the thinner branches, sometimes abrupt and dramatic changes in direction, occasionally staying so close to the other obvious branch that they're practically the same. In the cold air and in the condensation are a thousand invisible trees, each as beautiful and different as the other, and this twig is attached to every one. In a moment, they grow, dry, decompose, and never were all at once. And still there is one tree: seventeen offshoots, eight buds, twelve leaves, and a soft fur made of thousands of tiny wet hairs that shake in the stillness from the mere disparity of heat between the boughs and the hovering ground clouds. The steam of fresh growth wafts upward.

On looking back, I can see where one branch splits off, where another be-gins, where three separate. If I were to take the ant's route, however, from the trunk to the tip of this twig or any other, it is one continuous path—one way to get to the new growth. There is one other way, a slower but much more satisfying path, and that is from the twig into space. You have to recreate this path as you go by stretching and growing. Take the rush you get after a good jog, right when you step into a hot shower, add the fun of sliding down a banister or jumping three flights of stairs, and the utter contentment of waking up with a shivering stretch and a bellowing yawn, and it nearly compares. Tree growth is like lingering childhood in slow-motion—there's nothing more invigorating; and when the leaves begin to turn—it's like making love with the sun and the sky.

I used to want to snap. Crack! Just to get that feeling of a raw end in the air, to get the sap and the green flesh bubbling. I never did, but I always thought that if I could do that, I could change directions on the head of a sunbeam. Maybe so—but that sort of change won't grow back. There's only one way to go, and that's outward. It's the way to grow. Once you get to where you can look back, you'll see the offshoots. You'll even spot dates like rings on a trunk that are the celebration of birthdays and anniversaries.

You'll see where your life has changed.

Anonymous, Ojai, California

JUNE 2

Through the Wind

I Feel you. AND on the wings
of Doves I see you. You are
with Me when I need you and even
when I forget you. You're at my side like
a Friend, And live within me
like the beating of my
Heart. You will never leave me
      You are My God.

Brenna Waack

JUNE 3

When you carry me,
    I know,
When you're by my side,
    I know,
I can feel your presence,
    even when I'm not trying.
When I feel you're really not there,
    and I think you've left me alone,
I hear your voice calling out to me,
    and don't know what to think
Confused and scared,
    lost and alone,
Are the only words I believe.
But I look inside, and look to the Heavens
    and know that you are there.
Let it be known, that you're all around
    and will never let anyone down,
When I need you,
    when I don't think I do,
You're there to help me float,
    and to dry my tears and to rest my fears,
And to make me believe in myself.
Whatever you bring me to,
    You will bring me through,
You know my life,
    almost more than I do,
And know how to guide me through
    You will paint me a smile,
And it will brighten up my life,
    to know that it was worth the time.
I will pray like a prayer is never ending,
    and sing like there is Heaven on Earth.
Because when I smile, I pray,
And when I cry, I pray,
But you prefer it when I smile . . .

Emily Joy Welch

JUNE 4

Perhaps one of the least well-known of Christianity's holy days.

Everybody is asked to wear red.

Not all understand why, though.

This is the birthday of the church.

Every disciple suddenly could speak in foreign languages so that God's word might be spread.

Christ had ascended to heaven ten days before this day, but his lessons could still be taught.

Over three thousand people were baptized on that day.

Since then, it is celebrated every year fifty days after Easter Sunday.

This miracle was a great moment for those who wished to spread the joy of Jesus.

JUNE 5

Pause for Psalms—Psalm 27

Read Psalm 27.

What is the mood or tone of this psalm? What feelings are expressed? Do you understand the person who wrote this psalm? Can you identify a popular song, movie, or television show in which these emotions are explored? Choose a single verse or line from this psalm and spend some quiet time reflecting on it . . . or simply repeat it over and over again. Create your own words for this psalm. Here is one contemporizing of it.

Psalm 27

When they come to eat my flesh—
the false friends,
gossips and critics,
the business people,
politicians,
loan sharks, landlords,

and all those
who feast on famines . . .
when they come to eat my flesh—

I will not fear,
for you set me on a rock,
you hide me in a tent,
you light for me
a plain path . . .
you hold me in your love.

JUNE 6

Dear God,
May the rivers flow with the water from the sky above. Let the creatures
of the earth all rejoice. May the earth be scattered with the beauty of the
many colors of the flowers and trees. Bring happiness, harmony, and love to
the humans and animals that live upon the earth. Let the many days of
summer be blessed with your love and kindness. Amen.

Arianna Kadlub

JUNE 7

Prayer of a Parent at Prom Time

For the right date, booked early enough for pleasant anticipation . . .
God, hear my prayer.
For the right dress, that will be remembered forever,
and for the generosity of people who donate last year's dresses
to kids with fewer resources . . .
God, hear my prayer.
For safety planned by the young people themselves,
so I don't have to be an awful nag or stay awake all night . . .
God, hear my prayer.
For groups of friends attending together,
some in pairs, some as singles, fully welcomed,
and for the freedom of same-gendered couples to hold hands . . .
God, hear my prayer.

For great weather, relaxed teacher chaperones,
good music, and a sense of fun . . .
God, hear my prayer.
For a memory of one of the last lovely moments of youth
unmarred by accident, drunken fights, or broken hearts . . .
God, hear my prayer.

JUNE 8

Dear God,
How did you think to turn the dead, lifeless cold into a warm, blooming
area for all to look at and smile upon? As the sun gets stronger, it's time for
fun and playing. But the warmth is short indeed, as you take out your
palette and paint the trees. What a wonderful sight, but the paint gets worn
down. The leaves fall and soon you cover the land with your blanket of
comfort, so all the life can rest, until another year of creation. Thank you
for this beautiful world. Amen.

Sayre Wilson

JUNE 9

I love myself
except my knees
hair
stomach
thighs.

I love myself
except my anger
fear
shame
despair.

I love myself
except my failure
weeping
falling
loss.

God loves me
despite

me.

Ingrid, Somerville, Massachusetts

JUNE 10

This prayer is dedicated to David Sanders, who mentored me from 2001 to 2003. In June, he signed on with the Boston Red Sox, and I know that no matter where David's baseball career may lead him, he will continue to spread the love of God to young people.

Dear God,
I pray that every young person may be blessed with a positive influence in his or her life as an inspiration. I pray that in times of struggle, he or she may be blessed with a role model who will listen, advise, and guide. I pray that every young person may be blessed with someone who believes and cares for him or her and treats him or her like the priceless person he or she is. I pray that every young person may be blessed with a mentor that makes him or her feel exceptional by taking time from a busy life to be there. Most importantly, I pray that every young person be blessed with a friend who will bring them closer to you and your son, Jesus, such as David has done for me. Amen.

Daniel Gorton

JUNE 11

Prom Prayer

O Holy God, please watch over our kids on this night so that they may make it home safely. Help them to be strong so they may be able to resist the temptations of drink and speed and intimacy and being dared to do foolish things by others. Grant them the insight they need to know right from wrong. Amen.

Jeremy Mann

JUNE 12

A Baccalaureate Prayer, Class of 2003

LEADER: We lift up our prayers to you, O God.

RESPONSE: *Loving God, hear our prayers.*

LEADER: During this time of triumph, God, we lift up our prayers to you. Protect our classmates as we move beyond the walls of our own school. Keep safe those students who will pursue their education at home, in a big city, or in the rural countryside alike. Protect those who will go forth to serve their country to ascertain that democracy and liberty will always live in the world. We pray to you, most gracious God, that our world will achieve peace.

God, grant us the assurance that our contributions to society will make a difference, that they will improve the world in which we live.

Assure us, God, that we will hold close the lessons we have learned here and not forget the friends we have made. Help us to be aware of your presence at all times as you guide our paths and allow us to keep our friends close and in our hearts. Bless our parents and families, God, for all of their help and guidance through our childhood. May their ever-important influence continue to shape our lives.

Finally, God, protect us as we enter forth into a new chapter of our lives. Guide us through life's journey. Walk with us in the good times and carry us in the bad until we come home again. Amen.

God, hear our prayers.

RESPONSE: *We lift up our prayers to you, O God.*

Zachary Wilmer Reichenbach

JUNE 13

God, please watch over me on this,
my day of confirmation.
Please be with me as I become an adult
in the eyes of my faith
and my family.
I know I may always be a child of God,
that you will guide me and keep me always.
Even if I turn away from my faith,
you will be there.

I am afraid, God,
I am afraid of this changing faith
and what it means for me.
Help me to grow
and to love the change
that comes with confirmation of my faith.
Please be with me as I take this new step
in the light of your love
and acceptance,
in the eyes of my family
and my friends—
those who take this step with me
and those who choose a different path.

Thank you for this day, God,
for this chance to explore your love
and to renew myself in you.

Amen.

Ingrid, Somerville, Massachusetts

JUNE 14

Reflection of hope by a high school art teacher

One of my high school students died a few days ago when his friend ran a stop sign and their car was hit broadside. Our high school and community are grieving. I'm in awe of our young people, of their support of one another, and their willingness to forgive; of their acceptance, tenderness, and love. Through their grief they have reassured me that the future is bright. I pray for God to guide and protect them as they travel through each day. May the positive experiences and lessons of these past days stay with them—and with me—every day.

Barbara Noble

JUNE 15

Prayer

What is a voice?
A voice can be soft or loud.
A voice can be shaky, yet determined.
Voices can speak in languages such as
Spanish, English, German, Chinese.
A spoken voice may not be understood by the world as a whole.
Our language barriers
at times alienate brothers and sisters
throughout the world.
Fortunately we all speak the language of silence.

Silence can be so loud it is deafening,
yet it can be so peaceful as to
lull one into a moment of prayer.

God, help us speak through silence.
Voices can be small, large, Spanish, English, Chinese.
Voices can be unique,
and voices can share beliefs that are.

Please help us learn that no matter
how silent a person may be,
there is no such thing as a nonexistent voice.

Elena Mertus

JUNE 16

The Wind Is Singing a Song

The wind is singing a song
to me.
I extend my arms
and spread my fingers
wide into possibility.

I am conducting
an orchestra.

I close my eyes
and there I see
every color calling my name,
begging me to fly.

I ride the breeze
floating through harmonies
and sneak into melodies.
The notes tickle my belly
and make me laugh out loud.

Never was anything
as beautiful
as this.

I stretch out the song.
it fills everything
and makes the world around me
as light
as the moon.

I swim in the whirling
colorful tune
for I have no reason
to leave

I know I am welcome
for I was invited.

You are invited, too.
the wind sings a song
to you.

Christy Borum

JUNE 17

Bible Study—Miriam

Read Exodus 2:1–8.

1) Miriam became one of the greatest prophets of Israel. As a teenager she saved her baby brother's life. Have you been responsible to protect a brother or sister? Or been protected? What does that involve?

2) Miriam demonstrated courage by interfering in the Pharaoh's daughter's business. What event recently has taken your courage?

3) What could you do to help children near or far away?

PRAYER: God, give me both compassion and courage. Now that I am beyond childhood, help me reach out to those who are young, vulnerable, perhaps endangered or ill, whether that involves prophetic speech or putting myself on the line. Amen.

JUNE 18

Prayer for Summer

School is now over. For two months we're free.
This summer I need you. Please watch over me.
Help me to stay safe and do what is right.
Help me to keep busy . . . Hmmm. Maybe not quite!
Help me to remember to follow all "rules,"
Help me, O God, to prepare for more school.
Help me to hold dear all the things that you teach.
I love you, dear God—See you at the beach! Amen.

Kristi Ferguson

JUNE 19

God, I pray for all fathers young and old—those who are wonderful and those who make mistakes, and especially teenage dads who are too young to be responsible, but sometimes they try so hard to play with their kids. I am so glad my own father has been a model in my life—always there. Bless him for his love of me. I pray for kids and adults whose fathers have died or who don't live near their fathers. Be a father to them on this holiday. And especially for those who have difficult relationships—this is a tough day. Help them and love them. And God, thank you for Father's Day barbecues and summer fun.

Anonymous, Des Moines, Iowa

JUNE 20

Coach Me, Lord

Cool, freshly cut grass fills me with its sweet, earthy scent
as I step from the shadows into
the light.

Thank you, Lord, for the black drape, laden with diamonds over my head,
for this gentle wind tickling my face, sending strands of hair across my brow,
for the agility of my body, free from burden,
and soaring over hurdles and closer to your
heavenly gates.

It's just what I dreamed it would be,
energy like electricity sparking and shooting through
the air, pricking the hairs on my back.
Disks of beauty and wonder, burning bright,
illuminating the sky with their glory,
the dirt, rich between my fingers.
I sense it on my face, coating me in milk chocolate brown,
making me feel strong.
Your presence lingering in the air, touching my shoulders softly,
engulfing my glove.

I thank you, Lord, for the presence of my family at this moment,
their love overflowing
onto the field, infusing the flowers with happiness,

my gratitude I forever owe them and you, my Lord,
you are so wondrous,
so mighty,
so magnificent . . .

Please stay with me through this hour of battle,
keep my eyes keen,
my judgment sharp,
my mind free of hate and angst.

If we lose, give me the strength not to scream in rage and sadness.
If we win, give me the strength not to boast and gloat,
keep me from harm's way,
let me catch the ball,
hold me in your arms,
lift me if I fall.

Be with me as my heart beats out of my chest,
my breathing rolls like waves against the rocks.

Dana Canelli

JUNE 21

Prayer for a teenager looking for a first job

God, I pray for teenagers looking for that first job—not baby-sitting or shoveling or lawn mowing or chores for grandparents—that first treated-like-an-adult, rough, tumble, got-to-be-on-time, really ugly uniform, tired feet, always bored or too busy, "would you like fries with that?" first job. Bless the hunt, bless the employers, bless the parents who drop off and pick up, bless the crisp new paycheck, bless the "wings." Amen.

Anonymous (adult)

JUNE 22

Heavenly God, Your daughter is now seeking your protection as she steps into her teenage years. Help her to be like a snail with a protective shell. The shell to protect her vulnerability and unawareness. Please keep her safe but let her have fun and live life to the fullest. Amen.

Ally Mangan

JUNE 23

Dear God, bless us and keep us,
bless us and sweep us
into the dust bin
of your love.

Anonymous #2, Portsmouth, New Hampshire

JUNE 24

My heart was broken on the ground,
What it had lost will not be found.
The pain it brought had no avail,
The tears it caused left a trail.
Even though I was surrounded by many,
Near my heart there weren't any.
Crying, weeping, and all alone,
I learned to continue on my own.
No friends to help unburden the heavy load,
I plodded along the lengthening road.
God, help the outcasts—they taught me to pray,
But how could I when I didn't know the way?
I came to a river I had to ford
On the other side stood the Lord.
With one blink he was next to me,
Just as real as you or me.
He said, "Let me help you, I'll take your sack,
You shouldn't carry stuff this heavy on your back."
So I passed him my backbreaking load,
Hand in hand we flew over the water that flowed.
As we went I noticed to my surprise
that the sack was shrinking before my eyes.
My heart was lifted from where it had sank
And we landed gently on the other bank.
"I love you dearly," he said to me.
"Inside your heart is where I'll always be.
I remember choosing the color of your eyes
I had hoped that they would never need to cry.

Keep Faith in your heart and Hope in your hands
That way your spirit will conquer all lands."
I blinked again and could see him no more
But I'll believe in him forever, that is for sure.

Jaclyn Kregling

JUNE 25

Giving us

Overflowing

Delight

Just

Encourage

Sinners to

Unite with the

Savior

Special

Precious

Incredible

Reasonable

Insightful

Trustworthy

Adam and Ryan Schrote

JUNE 26

God, I hope you can help my friends, family, and coworkers find some patience in their hearts for me as I try to figure out exactly how this faith thing works. Not only am I new to it, in the past I had spent so much time renouncing it that I'm not always sure of what I actually think. I'm not always sure of what sect of Christianity I fit into, or even if that part matters at all. I have so many questions. Please help me to not get overwhelmed with worries about my faith, help me to simply accept faith and not be bogged down by details that I fear are starting to drive the people in my life crazy from my constant discussion of them. Please help them to understand that I am the same person I've always been—I haven't gone crazy, I'm not about to join a convent (though I totally admire and respect anyone who does, for the record), or run off to be a missionary (again a respectable and amazing calling). I am who I've always been, with the added bonus of the belief in one God, the Father, the Almighty, creator of all that is, seen and unseen, so on and so forth.

Elizabeth Randell

JUNE 27

Summer Prayer

Dear God,
Thank you for summer. Thank you for the sun. Thank you for water to fill a pool. Thank you for baseball, football, and basketball. Thank you for the hot weather, rather than our winters' cold weather. Thank you for the bikes to ride. Thank you for the mountains to hike.
Thank you, God.

Ethan Cody

JUNE 28

Prayer of a Pastor

Creator God, we pray for our youth these days who struggle for a glimpse of your light. Help us to be beacons of your love and the hope that we have in Jesus Christ. May we learn better how to inspire them to be the future

leaders of your realm. Guide us to listen to the wisdom and innocence and hope that they have for the future. Help us to welcome their creativity and not get in the way—assuming that we know a better way for the future. Help us to be open to the change that must come in our churches if the youth are to find their place among us. Help us to be the bridges between generations in order to create harmony for all in our churches, for the vision of shalom must begin with us.
Amen.

Pam Spain

JUNE 29

The Bigger Half

You and I are only small parts of the greater whole
Yet you and I can really make an improvement
Since we know it should be so much better
Everyone who feels there's nowhere to turn
will know some comfort
and everyone who thinks they're not worth the wait
Will see they're more important that they ever thought

Every now and then you meet that someone who shows you life again
And every now and then you realize that you possess
that very same life that you saw in them
You can change things that you see are wrong in this world
You decide between the war and the peace:
Which one do you want to continue?

Annie Lalish

JUNE 30

In the Alzheimer's wing
sits a woman cradling a doll
who stares at the tv set all day long.
Another clings to my arm when I pass one morning,
thinking me a nurse,
"can my friend stay for lunch?"

She is all alone.

I am alone as well,
and frightened of the future that appears here,
the Paloma Unit where both my grandfathers have come
(although we don't say it aloud)
to die.

They are not alone,
not like so many others
who wait all day
for memory to fail.

No, they are not alone—
my mother comes,
and my father,
almost daily now—
and on occasion,
when God is strong enough in me,
I venture to this room,
this hall, antiseptic
and forgettable.
I come to visit love
for moments of remembrance.

Maria I. Tirabassi

ROOM FOR YOUR THOUGHTS

July

JULY 1

Hide

You're hiding from troubles
Come out
Don't be afraid
Stand forward and make peace with your fears
Live the joys and tears of life
Live another day
You're hiding from troubles
Come out and stay

Johanna M. Bozuwa

JULY 2

World Peace

Dear Heavenly God, I pray that you continue watching over all of the countries of the world. I pray that you bless the countries in financial debt without an abundance of money and food. I pray for the countries at war, that they may put aside their differences and join arms in Christ. I pray that they join the fight to make it to heaven. Amen.

Keith Tigner

JULY 3

Recently I have been analyzing the way people in general pray. Praying is a touchy subject and everyone has strong feelings about how and why they pray. I mean no disrespect to anyone's beliefs when I say that it seems to me that a large majority of Christians, most likely with the best intentions, pray for the wrong reasons. Obviously I have no way to back myself up on my opinions; I won't pretend to be an expert on the books of the Bible or anything like that, because I'm not. I just mean to explain myself.

When I go through a day at school, I hear a variety of prayers. "God, please let me do well on this test," or "God, please let me make the team." It's hard to tell the sincerity of the students praying at that point but nonetheless they are prayers. Even when you go to church a large portion of the service is devoted to praying for family members who are in need. Prayers like these are the ones I intend on addressing.

As Americans and Christians, are we praying for what God might consider to be the "right reasons"? Our lives really have been blessed compared to those in so many parts of the world. Therefore is it right to ask God for more? Looking back I can recall feeling unwell and asking for prayers. Now when I think of those instances, even though they were few, I feel selfish and ashamed. The seventeen years I've been on this Earth have been better in all aspects than for millions of people who've been alive for two, three, or four times as long as I have, even when I'm sick. Any one of us can relate to a time when we really felt we were having a hard time. Honestly, are those occasions really even worth a prayer? So what that I didn't make the soccer team and now feel depressed, so what if my girl-friend broke up with me. Citizens in Somalia and Iraq need prayers to have a meal and to live another day.

My understanding of the basis of Christianity is one of sacrifice. Sacrifice to help our fellow human being, despite his or her religious beliefs and culture. Therefore, I am asking all Christians to remember what our religion is really about and the sacrifices made for us when they pray. I understand that certain instances require prayer. If dad is struck with cancer, or grandma passes away, by all means pray and let your faith return. Use that faith to then fight for others who need it.

Most people would agree that God does not know the same boundaries of time in days, hours, minutes, and so on. I do not attempt to debate this but I will say that if God does know time, I do not intend to ever use even a second of it for myself again.

Anonymous, Schnecksville, Pennsylvania

JULY 4

God's Love

You love us all.
You want us to love one another.
Some of us will hear your call.
To love everyone like sister, brother.
You will love us for our whole lives.
When we are hurting, you help us.
Your love will fill the holes in our lives.
You love us but we must love ourselves.
You tell us to love our enemies
and when we do so love,
we will be loved by our enemy.
You teach us to be like a dove
You teach us about peace
You teach us about love and happiness.
Some think your love was for lease,
but others know that your love
can only be given if we are willing
to accept it with happiness.

Robert Smith

JULY 5

Pause for Psalms—Psalm 46

Read Psalm 46.

What is the mood or tone of this psalm? What feelings are expressed? Do you understand the person who wrote this psalm? Can you identify a popular song, movie, or television show in which these emotions are explored? Choose a single verse or line from this psalm and spend some quiet time reflecting on it . . . or simply repeat it over and over again. Create your own words for this psalm. Here is one contemporizing of it.

Psalm 46

Be still—
God is a refuge.

Be still—
the waters are troubled.

Be still—
the earth melts.

Be still—
there is desolation,
chariots burn.

Be still—
and know that I am God.

JULY 6

Why is it that I only seem to pray when I need something?
I just realized that I only ever make time to talk with God when I have a
    favor to ask.
How terribly selfish this is of me!
Prayer should be a time of thanks and communication,
Not just a time to ask God to make miracles happen.
Prayer is an opportunity to spill your true feelings,
And know that someone is always there listening.
From now on I will make a promise to God.

I will pray to him on a regular basis, not only to ask his assistance in life,
But to thank him for all the wonderful things he has blessed me with,
And to have a deep conversation during which I speak from the heart
    whatever is on my mind.
I can't believe I never realized this before,
And I am looking forward to spending valuable time with our gracious God.

Kim Yencho

JULY 7

Prayer of a pastor before the funeral of a teenager

God, in your utmost tenderness, I ask your care of every young person who comes today to grieve and also those who stay away because they are numb or afraid to be embarrassed by tears, or because their parents don't think it's appropriate. Give each one blessing for the loss and inner peace at this breach of the invulnerability of youth.

I pray for parents and close friends that in the tundra of sorrow a small fire of hope be lit here for them to warm their hearts.

I ask as well for myself—the right words to evoke memories and give comfort, the ability to show my feelings but give everyone confidence that I can be in charge of this service and carry them all through it, and a little later private time and space to mourn. Amen.

JULY 8

Here is a prayer for our country:

The things you have made cover the earth, the sky, the universe. Everything we need to survive: food to eat, water to drink, air to breath, and clothing for cold weather. So, God, why have the people turned away? How can they not see that they need you to take care of them? Help the government turn back to you so that they can make good choices in all they do. Amen.

Amanda Bolstridge

JULY 9

Are you there, God?
Are you here at Silver Lake?
Will you bring us happiness?
Are you real or are you fake?

We see you in the trees
We feel you in the breeze
We smell you in the flowers
We can sense your awesome powers

Are you there, God?
We need you in our lives
Will you give us a sign
to help the world survive?

We believe in you and in you we trust
Even when it's hard
Live up to you we must

You are here, God
You are here at Silver Lake
You will bring us happiness
You are real and not fake.

"Are You There, God?" Conference 2003
Silver Lake Conference Center, Sharon, Connecticut

JULY 10

O God
Our loving God
You are our creator
The one
The only
Peace
We need peace
We need help
Please help
Try, please
We love you

We need you
I love you
I need you
Please, help
Amen

Tracy Benson

JULY 11

I wrote this song after returning from a trip in the summer of 2002.
I volunteered in an orphanage, and fell in love with this little girl named
Fania. I wrote this song after I got back to my safe, comfortable life here
in the United States.

Fania

I look into your eyes, and I wonder what you'll be
What will you become, what will those eyes see?
I wonder can you feel me, my arms wrapped around you tight . . .
Can you feel my warmth and love? It's the only thing that's right.

Your tiny shoulders will bear heavy loads,
Your pretty eyes will see things they shouldn't see.
Your little hands will not have much to hold,
Your sweet ears will hear of things that shouldn't be.

You cry as I let go, it's time, I have to leave.
How does God do this, does she try not to see?
I want to close my eyes, and not let this feeling in . . .
Let me enter my sweet world and forget just where I've been . . .

But I know, oh but I know . . .

Your tiny shoulders will bear heavy loads,
Your pretty eyes will see things they shouldn't see.
Your little hands will not have much to hold,
Your sweet ears will hear of things that shouldn't be.

I don't know where you are now,
In God's arms I know for sure . . .
Whether here on earth or in heaven,
I know he's with you my little girl.

Someday those tiny shoulders will feel no weight.
Someday those pretty eyes will see heaven's light.
Someday those little hands will hold something great,
Someday those sweet ears will hear of all that's right.

Emma Catlett-Sirchio

JULY 12

God, I pray for all the orphans of the world—that you'll send someone to hold them and love them—even if only for a little while. And I pray that you'll help us to do what we can to work for a world in which all children have the love and nurture and basic things they need. And please, God, wherever Fania is, let her know that she is loved, and that I think of her a lot. Amen.

Emma Catlett-Sirchio

JULY 13

Prayer watching young people in church

Heavenly God, bless these young people who enrich our lives. May they be led by our good example as we are led by yours. And may we be open to their ideas, energy, and enthusiasm. Help us all grow together, work together and bless each other, guided by your love. Amen.

Mary Taylor (adult)

JULY 14

The price of a good education these days

I learned about Bastille Day in history class
senior year
I think. It was something about a prison
and the French
I think.

We don't really talk about the French much
anymore. They are no longer the allies
we love to hate—or maybe,
they're exactly that.

We don't really talk about prisons much
either. They're full of people
who have fallen through the cracks,
people we take vengeance on, nothing more.

I learned about Bastille Day in history class
senior year
I think. It was something about forgetting what we've done
and who we've done it to
I think.

Maria I. Tirabassi

JULY 15

We all live different views.
Most of us get scared
because we might lose.

We get through because of you.

Many think they haven't feared.
But truth is they do.
Because they're scared.

We get through because of you.

I have feared before
I'm not afraid to tell the truth.
To tell the truth you have to soar.
And I'm a youth
But we can be stronger than before.
Just tell the truth.

We get through because of you
and
I get through because of you.

Diane Hodge

JULY 16

Bible Study—Jeremiah

Read Jeremiah 1:4–10.

1) Have you ever been tempted to use "I'm too young" as an excuse not to be involved with something? How did God respond to Jeremiah when he tried that excuse?

2) If God knows us so well—knows who we were even before we were born—can there ever be a reason to hide from God? Reflect on that thought.

3) Have you ever felt that God put certain words into your mouth that you would never have thought of saying yourself? What was the occasion?

PRAYER: Dear God, use me as a prophet . . . a young prophet, the best kind, to speak your words. Thank you for your tender, all-knowing love and your willingness to talk honestly with teenagers. Amen.

JULY 17

God, I want to thank you for the fireworks in my mind. Explosions of color—new realizations and revelations that shape who I am and who I will become. Thank you for this free-spirited summer of new friends, realizations, ideas, and growth. The deepest dazzling darkness lights my way and fills me with hope for tomorrow.

Bethany Bodengraven

JULY 18

Standing together, we watch strangers become friends.

Holding hands and lifting our voices, we learn how to open our hearts.

All may join this circle and be included in this dance.

Love entwines us and we grow together in this way.

Often times we may forget the hands that once were gripped in ours.

May they never leave our hearts though, even if they've left our minds.

JULY 19

A Prayer for the Many

Tonight
I am thinking of you.
All of you
who feel so lost
so unprotected
so forgotten.
You young adults
in third-world war-torn countries
whom we are supposed to be helping.
How can you look forward to college;
to marriage; how can you hope?
I am thinking of you.
You young children
who should be playing outside all day
on these beautiful summer days—
eating bugs, getting your first bee sting—
instead of lying in hospital beds,
wondering if you will survive another day.
Tonight
I am thinking of you.
You of all ages
trapped in your own mind
out of your own self-control
questioned, evaluated, diagnosed,
Judged.
I am thinking of you.
Tonight.
I am praying for you.

Annie Lalish

JULY 20

Thank you, God, for all the great things in my life and for the trees, flowers, animals, and plants you created to help us live. God, I also pray for my friend's neighbor because she is going through a tough time right now. Also,

I pray for all the soldiers in war in the Middle East. God, I saw you today in a small river. It reminded me of you because it was gentle enough to stand in and not get swept away but strong enough to carry a small branch in the current. Thank you for everything. Amen.

Stephanie LaQuaglia

JULY 21

A prayer for a week at church camp

Sweet and tender God, I humbly ask your blessing:

Be with our campers who travel to this holy place. Settle their hearts and minds during the journey down the dirt road, as you transport them from ordinary time to sacred time.

Be with our counselors and leaders waiting in cabins as nervous as the campers (but better at concealing their anxiety).

Be with our staff recovering from a week of giving and preparing for yet another week of giving. Bless them as they open their tired arms and turn from cleaning bathrooms to creating a divine welcome.

Travel the path of our laughter and tears, that in the mingling of souls we might come closer to you and our authentic self. Help us create a unique community of seekers. Open our hearts to uplift one another; to hear one another; to find Christ in one another.

Help us imitate Christ's going out and coming back:

Jesus left the crowds (the computers, the cell phones, and the television) to stop the noise around him. He went
    to the wilderness
    to a lonely place
    to the desert
    to the garden
    to the lakeshore
to pray

And always, he returned

to community

May we remember that you exist around and within us; in all things. Help us to liberate you from the white box of Sunday morning and remember the words of one camper: "Here at camp, we play with God all day."

God, may we adults remember that we have as much to learn and gain from these young people, as we have to teach and give. Give us courage to be the adults when it is required but to let our campers awaken the youthful playful self we have too long neglected.

And finally, God, keep us safe this week, physically and emotionally, that we might truly learn to love you, love ourselves, and love one another. Amen.

Bryan Breault (adult)

JULY 22

Dear God,
Thank you for the lakes that I love to swim in. I love gliding under the crystal clear water. It refreshes me and I am grateful for that. Amen.

Taylor Renaud

JULY 23

A Prayer for a More Loving World

Dear most holy and eternally gracious God,

We both thank and praise you for your wonderful creation, which we call home. This world that you have made, as a labor of pure love, is stunning and magnificent. Along with this world you created us, protect us, and unconditionally love us, yet we are flawed. It isn't in appearance that we are imperfect, for you have made us all unique and beautiful. Our faults lie within the way we treat each other. It seems as though people have forgotten how they're supposed to love each other. Love is understanding, acceptance, encouragement, and compassion. Help us to remember these things. All too often people get upset over minor material things. Please, dear Lord, teach us how to love again. Grace us with your knowledge, so that we may be able to love our neighbors as you have instructed us to do. Sometimes life gets really tough and love is the only cure to our problems, so please teach us to love more freely. Amen.

Carlie Cummings

JULY 24

Thoughts concerning relationships:
Sex doesn't necessarily mean love. For a meaningful and caring relationship, hold off on sex until you truly know and love the person.
It's worth it.
Communication and trust are the most important parts of a relationship.

Miscellaneous thoughts:
Though it may seem like the world is falling apart,
never forget that there are still good deeds and good people in the world.
Are you one of them?

Pray for me. I'm praying for you.

Richard Ashenfalder

JULY 25

Sometimes kids are super fun
And we all play out in the sun
Sometimes they are holy frights
And I pray with all my might—

Give me strength to keep my cool
Even when I look the fool
Keep me playing nice and fair
Though upon my nerves they wear—

And I simply must remember
One month more until September
When I can't stop all of their wailing
Next summer, I'm getting a job in retailing

JULY 26

When God comes calling, I'm on vacation.
When God needs my help, I'm in the shower.
When God asks a favor of me, I'm on the phone.

Dear God,
It's not you, it's me.
You deserve better.

Ingrid, Somerville, Massachusetts

JULY 27

All God asks is that we love, unprejudiced. This is not a grand task, but it is a noble one worth doing. If we all love one another, it won't even seem like work. It will be as natural as summer barbecues or going on a date or having a sleepover with all our friends invited. It won't be drama or heartache—it will be the joy of a summer night sky spent with those we love around the world.

Anonymous, Cambridge, Massachusetts

JULY 28

Prayer of a parent with a first-time driver

God, these are my worries: driving too fast, turning around to talk to someone in the back seat, icy road conditions, fog, somebody else having alcohol or drugs in the car, getting a ticket, another driver being drunk or falling asleep and crossing the center line, insurance rates, flat tires in lonely places, running out of gas in lonely places, carjacking, unwanted backseat intimacy, dents.

God, this is my fear: one loss of judgment leading to a fatal crash.

God, this is my embarrassment: my child hearing my worries as criticism.

God, this is my great pride and my hidden regret: my child is growing up, accepting responsibility, and becoming mobile without me.

Help me, God, to separate the real from the fantastical in my feelings, under-stand the kinds of influence I can and should exert on teenage behavior, and celebrate this young adult's receiving society's symbol of maturity. Amen.

JULY 29

A First-time Quilter's Prayer:
Trapunto God

My fingertips bled all summer, pricked
with needle and pin—an attempt
at piecing together myself with you,
and putting us down in cloth.

You unfolded me in a tent under sequoia skies
and I prayed
"love this like you love me
and it will be worth the tattered thumbs."

So when we finally lay beneath squares of mountain majestic,
pastel sand stained-glass—
we were a patchwork of crooked seamed
kisses for that "in remembrance of me" lucky love.

Maria I. Tirabassi

JULY 30

Sand that slips away from under my toes
as waves roll back out to sea,
the salt that sticks to my skin and tangles my hair,
the breeze that cools and refreshes,
and brings me the scent of the ocean,
the lulling sound of swells breaking,
then retreating from the shore.
Every time I return to the ocean
my body inhales deeply,
embraces the sound and taste and feel of it,
and I remember why I love coming home.

Sarah Fineberg-Lombardi

JULY 31

Dear God,

Thank you for this wonderful week at church camp. I made so many good friends and we had a dance party in our cabin that was awesome! We all sang and dressed up and the guys came over and we took tons of pictures. It was so much fun to be on the mountain again; it's never the same from one year to another, but it's good anyway. The people I meet are always cool and I don't feel like I'm judged the same way I am at school. Thank you for creating such a beautiful place where we can all be happy. Amen.

Horton Center camper, Gorham, New Hampshire

ROOM FOR YOUR THOUGHTS

August

AUGUST 1

Litany

As I walk up to church and the bells are ringing.
My country church is just the right size.

Small in numbers, but faithful through and through.
My country church is just the right size.

Our abundance of love is priceless compared to any amount of money.
My country church is just the right size.

Whether you're four or ninety-four, you'll leave with the free treat of love.
My country church is just the right size.

Diane Hodge, Deer River Sunday School

AUGUST 2

Summer

live
imagine love
play music
laugh always
dance silly
grow with me
my friends

Kimberly Hughes

AUGUST 3

Prayer for the city

Hello, City

Pray for asphalt.

I stare into skyscrapers
and see God winking back
in the setting sun's reflection.

Pray for chainlink fences.

I walk the streets
and the strange faces
shine God's love unceremoniously.

Pray for dank alleys.

I see the stars
dimmer here, but they still recall
God's wonderment.

Pray for me.

I hear sirens
and I am afraid for the safety
of all God's children.

AUGUST 4

How can I not?

This natural beauty I cannot comprehend
To have been created by seven days' end
Illuminating sunsets, vibrant purple pink
Sweet warm rain, the beauty makes me think
Of you, way up high, thinking of me
I wonder if it weren't for you, where I'd be?
Shimmering, shining, clear blue lake
This perfection nearly makes my soul ache
Hidden, healthy, deep, deep trees
Summer's stillness brings me to my knees
My thanks and praises to you for this day
Overwhelm me—how can I not stop and pray?

Annie Lalish

AUGUST 5

Pause for Psalms—Psalm 14

Read Psalm 14.

What is the mood or tone of this psalm? What feelings are expressed? Do you understand the person who wrote this psalm? Can you identify a popular song, movie, or television show in which these emotions are explored? Choose a single verse or line from this psalm and spend some quiet time reflecting on it . . . or simply repeat it over and over again. Create your own words for this psalm. Here is one contemporizing of it.

Psalm 14

The fool says, "There's no God,"
then eats the poor like bread.
Which is the greater
wickedness—
the disbelieving tongue
or the cruel sharp teeth?

For me . . . I fear the chewers,
the awful gnawers of life,

who roast the oppressed
on spits of money,
who fry the ghetto child,
grind the bones of the rural poor.

AUGUST 6

Hiroshima

O God
we remember . . .
No, we don't remember.
Our grandparents do,
some of our parents,
and all of the Japanese . . .
Let ours be a generation
that folds cranes
in the heart.

Anonymous, Des Moines, Iowa

AUGUST 7

Prayer for a teenager having a baby

God, I pray for teenagers having babies. I affirm the choices of a young woman to carry forward a pregnancy even as I affirm the other choices she could have made. I invite grace into the decisions she will yet make—about adoption, single parenthood, or marriage. I ask your presence in lonely evenings of doubt, fear, and hope, your strength during hours of labor, your steadiness during the first bath, the first pediatrician visit, the forty-fifth night of broken sleep.

I call the blessing of Joseph upon the young man who will face in some way the ambiguous responsibility of young fatherhood. Make clear his next steps.

I intercede for families, support agencies, doctors and nurses, churches, high school day care centers—that all may offer wise and compassionate care.

I pray for a close circle of friends willing to help—by not excluding from social events, and by offering free baby-sitting.

I lift into your heart like a manger the child of teenage parents—status symbol or embarrassment—who may experience a multigenerational family, be raised by grandparents, or know the intense emotions of adoptive parents and eventual meeting with birth mother, who may be an only child or one of many siblings, who will need more than many others your baptism on the inside whether it happens on the outside or not. Swaddle this new life with unconditional love. Amen.

Anonymous (adult)

AUGUST 8

We know, God, that each choice we make in life
affects more than just our own.
That even the tiniest gesture made
can help tip the balance between
talking about a better world,
and achieving that better world.
Please help us to be a better part of this global community.
To make decisions that will help not only ourselves,
but others around us and those who will come after us.
In your name we pray
Amen.

Shane Mathews

AUGUST 9

Dear God,
Let all families be safe and let every person have a family to come home to and spend time with. Don't let Evan fall off the stone wall. Keep Mylo safe—don't let Chester hurt him. Keep Dad supple and Mom springy. Thank you for keeping my brother safe while he's riding his bike. Thank you for my almost wonderful family—although I wish my brother and sister and I could get along better. I pray for my family to hold together until I get back. I pray for these people who love me no matter what I do

simply because they're family. My family is not only my sister, father, brother, mother, but those who care about me the most. We all need family, even if she's criminal or he's homeless—whether they're friends from summer camp we've only just met or the people who have always been with us. My family is good to me, so please let them feel happiness and peace. Thank you, God, for giving us families who love us and care for us through sickness and grief, through happiness and laughter, and forever. Amen.

Jacob Renaud, Aubrey Voigt, Cassie Spencer, Cameron Moore, Carl Ezyk, Mary Cliche, Sanne Brown, Chris Connelly, Tucker Tirey

AUGUST 10

Hot Summer Job

My job is the same every day—never any action
It's the beginning of August and I'm already bored
Knowing I still have a month of this job is such a distraction
I try to pay attention to you but my thoughts go to my bucket and mop
I mentally complain about my job
Although I know my life is really great
With my thoughts of self-pity it gets hard to keep you on top
The bottom line is that when I die I know my fate
So give me the strength to follow you God
Help me to persevere so I can clearly see you
Make prayer time so consistent it'll never seem odd
I'll show my love is true

Greg Kelley

AUGUST 11

Dear Heavenly God,
Please help me to live my life as you see fit. Allow me to take in the troubles and pain of everyday life and learn from them. Help me to know that I am not alone in this world. Please help me to put more faith and trust in you. Thank you for everything you have given me, good and bad; they have all molded and shaped me into who I am. Amen.

Kasi Smith

AUGUST 12

Elemental Gloria

There's a day in the middle of summer when tar ripples mirages in a heat-laden black wave. The sky's ripped open with no clouds in sight; the earth chokes on its own dust-filled mouth and spits out wilting sunflowers from between its jaws.

On this day, sparrows flap tiredly from nest to dirt, and only the crickets muster any enthusiasm for the celebration of life. Their rubbed wings glorify all that may be seen, smelled, tasted from the earth—all that may be touched and heard and carried on the winds.

This is the land singing sweet hallelujahs to drowsy mother and child, to caress of lovers' gaze, to guide all who breathe and play and work to come forth and rejoice in this gift of a renewing and patient mothering earth.

Ingrid, Somerville, Massachusetts

AUGUST 13

Dear God,
We thank you for the wonderful time we've had this week and for bringing us together under you, just as you brought together the people at Pentecost. Help us to keep our faith even when people make fun of us, and help us to do what we think is right. And help us to keep the friendships that we've made this week. Amen.

Kristin Zukowski and camp friends from "God is still speaking" Oceanwood

AUGUST 14

Prayer for the time of transition from high school to college

Most Loving God, you have provided me a home, and a place of worship in which I feel so loved. Everyone knows my name and I am always invited to share my ideas and my joys and my concerns without fear. Now I am going to college away from the security of my family, friends, and church family. I do not know how I will be received. I am not sure if my views will be affirmed or even tolerated. I am not sure if I myself will be accepted for the way I look. The one thing I do know is that your love, Lord, and the love of my family and church family will go with me in spirit. No one can take that love away from me. However, sometimes when things happen, I tend to forget who I am and how much I am loved. Help me, please, O God, to be reminded of that abundant love and give me courage to walk faithfully in new situations. In the name of Jesus my Savior I pray. Amen.

Rev. Linda Miller-Pretz

AUGUST 15

Early Morning Summer Prayer

What better time to pray
Than at 6:30 A.M. on the beach?
On this August morning before the heat arrives
There's just a touch of breeze
The crash of the waves reminds me of your unstoppable love
The blue sky above makes me yearn to be in your presence
Bless this time that I may use it wisely
A fine prayer session without distraction
Just God and I
Shall begin at 6:31

Greg Kelley

AUGUST 16

Bible Study—Timothy

Read 2 Timothy 1:1–7.

1) Timothy is a young apostle who grew up with his mother and grand-mother as models of faith. Who are your models?

2) Do you ever feel "burned out?" What would you ask God to "re-kindle" in you?

3) Paul's letter meant a lot to Timothy and to those of us who have been reading it ever since that time. To whom could you send an encouraging letter or e-mail?

PRAYER: God, take away my spirit of cowardice. Even though I feel weak, even unpopular, give me a spirit of power. Even though sometimes I think no one loves me, give me a spirit of love for others. Even though self-discipline these days is only used for athletics, give me a spirit of self-discipline in my faith life. Amen.

AUGUST 17

God, you are helpful and and caring. I thank you for my parents, brothers, dog, cat, and great friends. You are full of forgiveness and have mercy on us all. I try to do good things for others because of your love for me. Also, I think you are wonderful because you help people overcome their sicknesses. Amen.

Caroline MacIntosh

AUGUST 18

God Keeps Us Cool

The hot sun of August beats down upon me
I roll out of the driveway and head for the beach
No longer will I be sweating when I splash into the sea
The refreshing Atlantic is not far from reach
Now I'm cooled down but my throat's dry
Yet this is solved by lemonade so fresh it's almost tart
With another sip I remember God's supreme love with a happy sigh
And know that the worst heat we escape by accepting Jesus into our hearts
Praise be to the Lord
Who will always keep us cool

Greg Kelley

AUGUST 19

Even though I might sometimes
get annoyed with my friends and yell . . .
Thank you, God, for just those friends,
I pray that you treat them well.

Even though I might sometimes
be embarrassed by my mom and dad . . .
Thank you, God, for my parents—
some family situations are sad.

Even though I might sometimes
call my sister a bad name . . .
Thank you, God, for those people
who listen to you just the same.

Even though I might sometimes
get mad at you for reasons unknown . . .
Thank you, God, for helping me
find the light you've always shone.

Betsy DuFault

AUGUST 20

Dear God,
Thank you for not letting my friends and family get hurt or killed in the storm, Isabel. It's a blessing because many people were hurt and had trees fall on their homes or their cars. Some people's whole houses collapsed. There were more than one million people without lights. I feel blessed, and I thank you for not letting my family and friends get injured. In Jesus' name, amen.

Denzel Perry

AUGUST 21

Prayer of a parent who has made mistakes

Dear God, hear the prayer of a prodigal parent.
I have made mistakes.
I have failed to trust or foolishly trusted my child.
I have been unfairly angry
and lied even as I have demanded truth.
I have interfered with relationships and pushed
my own athletic, academic, college or job agenda,

rather than investigating and fully respecting
my child's gifts and interests.
Sometimes I have turned off music,
and sometimes I have turned off listening.
I have modeled dishonest behavior—
with speed, with alcohol, with taxes—
and guided my actions by
selfishness or acquisitiveness.
Then I am shocked and ashamed looking
into the mirror of a young face.

God, help me understand how to say, "I'm sorry,"
how and when to change,
how and when to have faith that you heal and repair
the wounds and shattered axles of our relationships.
For I do believe that you turn
the hearts of parents to their children
and the hearts of children to their parents.*
Amen.

*Malachi 4:6

AUGUST 22

Dear God in Heaven,
You have blessed me with love.
You have blessed me with health.
You have blessed me with opportunities to be all I can be.
And I thank you.

Please let me remember those who are not loved.
Please let me remember those who are not well.

And let me serve you by being a friend to them who have so much less
    than me.
Let me serve you by providing those who have so little with my help,
    my time, and my caring.

Please continue to give us a chance to spread your word to others so we
    might all become a more caring world of people.

Ashley Miller

AUGUST 23

Believe

In the

Book

Like it is your

Eternity

Caring

Helping

United together

Reassuring

Coping with one another

Hopeful

Adam and Ryan Schrote

AUGUST 24

A prayer for a fearful freshman

How many nights did I lie awake, God,
wondering if I had packed the right clothes,
if the music I listened to was cool enough for college,
or if my roommate would be laughing at me behind my back

I worried about it all,
whether my professors would expect me to write fifty-page papers
or read entire textbooks in a week,
and nothing would ease my mind

Every time I lay down to sleep, panic would creep under the covers
and I would press my hand against the wall
to the room where my parents lay with their own fears
for my future

How many hot summer nights did I lie awake, God,
how often was I still awake to greet the dawn?
How did you comfort me, God, when I cried out that last summer home,
how were you there through the darkest nights
so that I knew, those nights under the stars, there was nothing to fear.

AUGUST 25

Dear God,
I ask for your blessing today to help everyone in need. Every day there are
thousands of people with different kinds of problems; some may be big or
small problems. Please help them overcome them in any way you can. You
have the power that can heal anything or anyone. And today we ask that
you use it for the people in need. You are our Father and Holy Ghost. We
ask you to touch the ones who don't know you and show them the holy
path. In your name, Amen.

Alex Martin

AUGUST 26

Flying high
in the midnight sky
watching all the
stars that pass us by
Steering on a jagged end
watching clouds
that seem so thin
dreaming of many
precious things

thinking of times gone
by
Homeward bound we sail a
ship into the starry sky.
For
we still have many
dreams to dream and
many ships to
fly!

Joi Ward

AUGUST 27

There is a rock.
It is a rock but it was lava.
It is a rock but will it become sand? Will it become mud?
Forgetting its past, allowing its future, the rock embraces itself.

Sam Roden

AUGUST 28

For A Child Going Abroad

We gave you roots and now you take wing
As you fly from us to go abroad.
We revel in your independence, your abilities and autonomy,
Yet we want to embrace you, safe in our arms.

Hold us close in your heart as you race towards new things,
Remember that as much as we miss you, we love you.
We pray you will return home unharmed,
More mature, wiser, experienced, open to new things.

Ellen Fineberg (adult)

AUGUST 29

A song to be sung.

A tale to be told.

Undoubtedly bursting forth,
unstoppable—gaining strength
and force.

A taste to be sensed.
Taste this fruit of the good life—
sharing the wonder of the world.

All so simple; and yet,
we cloud up our lives.

Step back, gain control
and find the above so
simple that it is as
a single strand.
No knots to worry you,
nothing to come unraveled,
simply one solitary strand
of feeling—keeping your
heart and mind as one.

Olin Johannessen

AUGUST 30

Dear God,
We pray for peace in our world.
We pray for unity and acceptance among those who are different.
We pray for others, who need your guidance in their lives at home,
    at school, or at work.
But most of all, we pray for your presence in our lives. Amen.

Andrea Kautz

AUGUST 31

until the sun stops to shine
you have always made me belong
you are who holds my hand
to guide me through my day
and to help me understand
what life may bring along the way
you are my God my only one
and you show me that dreams can come true
so thank you God for everything
I know I will always love you

Kate Nuschke

ROOM FOR YOUR THOUGHTS

September

Dear God,

Thank you for my summer fun.

For our awesome camp, our new boat, and the gorgeous pond and its
beautiful surroundings.

For your creation of loons and their baby loon.

Thank you for tubing with friends and family.

The fun of jumping from tube to tube, flying over waves, and doing
"double donuts."

Thank you for helping me learn to water-ski and slalom-ski.

It was you who gave me the strength to get up and become good.

Thank you for our neighbors and all our friends.

I had a wonderful summer, Lord, and you are to thank for all of it.

Thank you, God.

Amen.

Lauren Fowler

SEPTEMBER 2

A Late Fee Prayer

God, when I worked at the video store,
it felt like everyone who came in looked down on me for being there.
It was just a summer job—four months so I could pay
at least some of my own way—
but every shift was a test of pride.

Red polo shirt, garish yellow nametag—this was the wrong end
of retail to be working in this town.
Video rental was not prestigious enough,
there were no perks,
except, maybe, the air conditioning on a muggy morning.

I was less than dirt, God, less than anything, not
worthy of respect from people who rented porn at 10 A.M.,
and that hurt. It stung even though I knew these people were wrong,
even though I knew how hard I had worked all my life
to be considered something special.

It was the lack of eye contact, the distracted air
of the girls I'd known in high school
and the snide stares of those who felt they'd waited too long in line
that reinforced every self-consciousness I had risen above.

In this retail isolation, however,
I found dignity, God. I found myself standing taller,
forcing "thank you's" on deaf ears,
letting the pain trickle off of me
in florescent light of a job well done.

SEPTEMBER 3

Dear God,
Today is my first day of school and I am really nervous. It's a new school
with new people that I haven't met yet. God, please watch over me and give
me the strength to meet a new friend. Amen.

Meghan Krato

SEPTEMBER 4

God is our hope
through sickness and doubt.
God is our friend,
when all others run out.
God is our peace,
when Earth goes to war.
God is our love,
for forever and more.

Meredith Grubb

SEPTEMBER 5

Pause for Psalms—Psalm 6

Read Psalm 6.

What is the mood or tone of this psalm? What feelings are expressed? Do you understand the person who wrote this psalm? Can you identify a popular song, movie, or television show in which these emotions are explored? Choose a single verse or line from this psalm and spend some quiet time reflecting on it . . . or simply repeat it over and over again. Create your own words for this psalm. Here is one contemporizing of it.

Psalm 6

So sad I make the bed swim.
From weeping my bones wax old.
Grief is toxic
and sorrow punishes
the body wracked by crying
of the child of God.

Heal me soon.
My faith and my spirit are strong
but my eyes fall out,
my bones are snapping,
my days are draining away,
and, after I die, God—
who will sing to you
my bright, bright song?

SEPTEMBER 6

Dear God,

Well, high school is going fine so far. But I know that there will be ups and downs along the way. I have a whole four years to go! That's going to be a while. But in a way I'm happy, because that means four years with friends and family. I know I'll have some bad days, nothing can stop that. I just wish I'll have a good experience. I know I'll get all the support from my parents. I'm really glad you're going to always be there with me. So I guess in a way I can't wait for all the year to come.

I hope Mary's having a good time in college. I don't know how I'll leave here in four years. This church is really special and my friends and family will all be gone. But that's the way life is supposed to be. You'll eventually have to leave the ones you love. I hope when I grow up, that I'll have a good church and community to go to. My parents are lucky they did. I'm proud it's this one.

I don't really know if people think about things as much as I do. I really like to cherish moments. I feel a special feeling when I'm in some place very special to me, like the D's house. I wish they'd never left but, like I said, that's life. You have to deal with the things thrown at you. Well, God, wish me luck on this year. I hope it's one to remember and so are the years to come. I know you'll always be there for me. Peace out. I'll talk to you later.

Paul Jamison

SEPTEMBER 7

Prayer of a teacher

Hunched over papers, they see black and blue on white.
God, as they lift up their heads, what do they hope to see?
    Show them, whisper to them, the answers, God.
        Put the writing
            on the wall,
            on the blackboard,
            on the windshield, God.
They are looking, God. Show them your face.
    Help them write——— in bold letters and bright colors
        statements that ring with faith.
        dramas and dreams that inspire
        epistles that pursue truth

Draw them closer to you, be the subject of all searches.
And that empty line at the bottom of the page—
                    show them your signature.

Dianne Prichard

SEPTEMBER 8

(To be read aloud with "rap" style.)
Dear God,
I know you love me and you know I love you too,
from the tip-top of my head to the bottom of my shoe.
You help me when I'm weak, and you help me when I'm late,
and I know you're the only one that will ever know my fate.
From 6 A.M. to 12 P.M., you're always by my side,
whether inside, outside, all side, no side, even in my pride.
Whenever I am calm, and whenever I fret,
You will be by my side, and on that I'll make a bet.
Through the wind and through the storms,
Through the pain and through the gain,
I know you'll be right there, even if I was lame.
Through cold, dark nights, and hot, bright days,
I know you are the one who stays.
Through school and church, through church and school,
I know you are the one that will help me keep cool.
Out of my mother's womb, to my last minute,
I know you are the one that will be through all of it. Amen.

Jacob Butler

SEPTEMBER 9

Dear God,
All of our friends are here today because of you. You've blessed us with
    them and this wonderful trip. Please bring us closer together and teach
    us to respect one another. Amen.

YAKS youth, grade 6–8, Somers Congregational Church UCC, Somers, Connecticut

SEPTEMBER 10

In God's Eyes

Completely securely trapped
This place is full of farcical
People who cry for peace but don't think
To change their own ways
More entranced by which celebrity
Is currently in a scandal
Too worried about their own relationships
Too caught up
In our country's still-wealthy economic slump
To look at the truly desperate.
We've got items on our "to do list"—
Concern self with self.
Why should we rescue foreigners—
because there's no such thing
As humans being foreign to other humans
And country boundaries mean nothing
In the Eyes of God
And we're still the same

Annie Lalish

SEPTEMBER 11

Future Hope

In loving memory of those who perished on September 11, 2001.
In thanks to all who are risking their lives and to those who have lost their
lives to protect our families and freedom.

Sweltering, hot, breathless sky
Longing for the clouds to cry

Loss of friends; shattered love
Angered lands; stained with blood

Fire burns within our souls
Will it quench? No one knows

Smoke and ash blot out the sun
Darkness falls on everyone

Tears run down a smoky face
Staring at this empty space

A hush, a silence, a crash, a scream
Blood runs cold as wintry streams

Hatred like an angry beast
On innocents was sent to feast

Where pillars once reached heavenward
Ruin in its wake now stood

And yet, the light of hope remains
A healing balm to ease our pain

It's from the very depths of gloom
That love and joy spring forth to bloom

Our earth in peace will we learn?
Now the time has come to turn

The sun as our guiding light
Bears us through the dark of night

A world united ever more
On wings of peace mankind will soar

Kaleigh Lambert

SEPTEMBER 12

Dear God,
Your loving child searches for courage to go on her journey through the sky. She dreams that she will not go but fears she will never get to her destination before something terrible happens to innocent lives that shouldn't be taken off this planet. Amen.

Lynnea Nikiforakis

SEPTEMBER 13

Praying, for me, is a way to vent. I see God as a friend always there for me. The more and more I think about God the more I get confused. Why were wars started over God? I know Christianity and the actions that are caused by it are different. But why? I pray for answers to all these unanswered questions. Why does God forgive us always? When September 11 occurred my thoughts of God and religion changed for the better and the worse. Does God really want praise? I struggle with this a lot. Why do people die? Is it to prove a rule? On September 11 many people died innocent or not. Why create something you are going to destroy? Life is indeed short. We grow, we learn, and we love. But what is the point of life? Does God put us on earth for a set of reasons? I want, no, I need to know why. If God has all power, how come people die who are close to you. I miss them. I pray for answers. I pray for a reason. I pray for family. The extent of praying has no limit. She died last week. Why? That's all I ask. If you're out there, please tell me. I want to know, I yearn to know, I need to know. Why? If there is any reason. Are you there? If indeed we are friends, why do I not trust you? I don't close my eyes when I pray—why?

Jeff Long

SEPTEMBER 14

Prayer of a Confirmation Teacher/Mentor

God—Con-firm my foundation.

As I begin this confirmation program as a teacher (mentor)—
help me to share my excitement about the Bible,
my depth of spirituality and
real examples of how it sustains me,
(in fact, God, help me to be a little more spiritual
while these kids are watching me),
my knowledge about Church history,
my pride in our denomination,
my openness to our neighbors in world religions,
and my grappling with my own ethical decisions
and the decisions that young people make.

As they are learning, guide me to learn something new.
As they are growing, stretch my roots and bud-tips;
When they wrestle with questions,
evaporate the easy answers on my lips,
and, whether I have taught these concepts
ten, twenty, forty years, or this year for the first time . . .
bring me with enthusiasm and humility to
God's holy power-point presentation . . .

the con-firmation of our faith. Amen.

SEPTEMBER 15

Dear God,
The prayer I want to use is—that I pray that whatever happened on 9-11-01
will not come back. It was a disaster for many of us. I pray that no more
war will be done. War shouldn't happen. I also pray that the people who are
sick, who have cancer and any kind of sickness, that they could find a cure,
and that they get well. Amen.

Emily Jeffris

SEPTEMBER 16

Bible Study—Eutychus

Read Acts 20:7–12.

1) Eutychus got so bored in church that he went to sleep and fell out the window. Have you ever felt that bored in church?

2) Everything stopped when Eutychus had his accident. Do you agree that what happens to one teenager is more important than any church program or business agenda?

3) Paul was a boring preacher but he held Eutychus and brought him back to life. What adults around you are "holders?"

PRAYER: God bless our church that it may be a place of relevance, renewal, and resurrection. We remember your love for each individual. If I'm the one who notices that someone has disappeared from church or youth group, help me do something about it. Amen.

SEPTEMBER 17

Peace. Love. War. Hate. Terrorism. I sum them all into one word. Drama. I hate war. Which, I know, everyone does. Yet we go to war. As you read this, I want you to remember, this is all my opinion. So please don't come to me and tell me I am wrong. You are welcome to your opinion, just as I can have mine. Some of the things may make you angry. Some you may agree with. But remember, this is just what I think, it isn't anyone else's words but mine. Here is a question to think about: is war really worth all this trouble? Now, with that in mind, I will begin.

On September 11, 2001, terrorists flew two planes into the Twin Towers. One crashed near Pittsburgh, Pennsylvania. Another into the Pentagon. I have visited the Flight 93 crash sight near Pittsburgh. The feeling I got there was like nothing I have ever felt before. As I looked at the memorial, I began to feel so horrible for the families of people lost that day. There was one in particular that touched me. A girl my age lost her father. She wrote him a poem, and it was posted on his angel statue there. But another thought came to my mind. Why did it take a tragedy for everyone to come together? Everyone had American flags out for a few months after it happened. Slowly, they began to disappear. Now, you see one once in a blue moon. I am not the most patriotic person in the world, but I think it is pathetic when people come together for a short time, then just forget it all.

What the terrorists did that day was a horrible thing. In fact, horrible isn't even a good word to describe it. You can use every word you know to describe it, but none of them are adequate for what they did. They are the most heartless people I have ever come across. They kill people and don't care. How can anyone be so awful? It is a question that may never be answered. Now, here is a question for you: by going to war, aren't we stooping to their level? Our troops try not to bomb the innocent. But, by going to war, aren't we doing their dirty work for them? They don't care who dies. They will sacrifice anyone and everyone. We are putting our brave people out there, to do the terrorists jobs. I really don't understand the point of war.

Countries fight each other; one wins. In the process, hundreds of people die. What do we do when it is over? Wahoo, we win the war, now what? We control the Middle East? They don't seem to back down too easily.

Basically, I think war is pointless. Let them hate us. By going to war, we are egging them on. We are telling them, come get us.

What they did to us was horribly wrong, but all we are doing is letting them succeed. They want us to die. They want our people dead. Our soldiers are dying. Their plans are working.

In my opinion, they did those things so we would fight them. Their leaders have outsmarted us so much it's sickening. And America continues to fight. Just losing more and more people. When will this all end?

Is war really worth all this?

Amanda Nickles

SEPTEMBER 18

Peace is

Quiet
Caring
Loving
Sharing
Graceful
Willing
Risky
Chilling
Peace is God!

Felicia Fowler and Sarah Heath-Howe

SEPTEMBER 19

Treasure the Memories

Yesterday they were here.
Now they're gone.
Teary-eyed we stand,
Not wanting it to be true.
We loved them and
They loved us.
It's not fair.
We should be immortal,
Or at least we and everyone we love
Should disappear from here at the same time
To spare each other the pain
And sorrow
And heartache
We now have to go through.
It's hard, I know.

They say time shall heal all wounds.
I'm not sure that that's true.
It can help,
But losing someone you love,
That can never be gotten over.
We all wish they were here again,
Standing beside us,
Smiling.
It's hard not to think of
The time we can't share.
Of all that should have been said and done.
But that's in the past,
It's over now.
And guilt will just add to our pain.
We're human,
We make mistakes.

Just think of the good times you shared.
Remember the days you went to the beach,
Or toasted marshmallows over the fire.

The rainy days you spent baking cookies (and you got to lick the spoon!),
And when you talked endlessly and they listened,
Even though they probably had much better things to do.

They let you cry on their shoulder,
And let you rant and rave over a bad grade
Or a fight with your best friend.
Just remember the days,
And forgive yourself for the bad ones.

For the gone are not gone,
You just can't see them or talk to them.
They will always live forever in your heart.
And you'll see them again soon enough.

Treasure the memories and they will never truly be gone.

Katherine Gill

SEPTEMBER 20

God,
Thank you for helping Grandpa Jim to get a little better. Please help
Mrs. Del Isola to get better also. Please help me to do well in school and
not get lost too much. Help me to get better friends than I had last year
and not make me have bad experiences such as I did last year. Bring peace
to the world and keep people safe. Amen.

Jill Murphy

SEPTEMBER 21

Prayer of a Director of Child and Family Services

Dear God,
Our children need you even when they can't find you in their midst. Please
surround them with your love and guide them with your presence. Stand by
them as they struggle with right and wrong, with the many temptations of
adolescence and with the pressure to "go along with the crowd."

As their parents, coaches, and teachers we ask that you guide us as well. Our children are our most precious gifts and we have been given a daunting task in raising them to follow in your footsteps. Please hold us close and provide us with the strength, compassion, and resilience to nurture and support them even when they push us away. We are humbled and awed by the challenges and joys of raising and mentoring children, Lord, and ask for your love and guidance in this and all things. Amen.

Shari Landry

SEPTEMBER 22

Rain in Autumn

The leaves upon the trees,
Though beautiful and bright,
In a clear day's sunlight,
Are now dark and damp,
Silhouettes against a sky dark as night.

Brendan McCann

SEPTEMBER 23

A Prayer for my Great-Grandmother

Dear God,
I want to say a prayer for my great-grandmother. She is ninety-seven years old and she had a stroke and she is still recovering from it. I would like you to help her through her recovery and return her to her home safely. I pray this in the name of Jesus Christ. Amen.

Sarah Wilkins

SEPTEMBER 24

School shouldn't be a place we're afraid.

Columbine changed that for many of us.

How children's sorrow could go unnoticed for so long is a terrible mystery.

One day altered the world and we heard their cries at last.

One day changed us all and we can never go back.

Let all who see sadness and pain seek to help those who need our love
the most.

SEPTEMBER 25

The Trees of Autumn

Beautiful, colorful are the trees,
As they rustle in a light autumn breeze.
Soon to the ground they will drop their leaves,
But for now they rustle in a light autumn breeze.

Brendan McCann

SEPTEMBER 26

O dear God,
Thank you so much for this wonderful season. Fall—I love it! So many
beautiful colors. That first pile of leaves I raked up is going to be so much
fun to jump into. O thank you, God, for that great smell of leaves. It makes
my day to know that you made such a wonderful season. Thank you.
Amen.

Tracy Benson

SEPTEMBER 27

God Was There

God is not always seen or heard, but when we need it the most, we can feel that God is there.

I had a fun-filled day and went home that night in good spirits. As I pulled into the driveway, I got the feeling that things were not right. Thoughts that saddened me, thoughts that I was ashamed of even thinking, and thoughts that were feeble attempts at reassuring myself that everything was fine. I went inside and was greeted by tear-stained somber words saying that there had been an accident. Nothing was known accept that he was at a distant hospital in intensive care and my parents had gone to be with him. There was nothing I could do except try to sleep because I had school the next day. Once again thoughts began running through my head, and they were filled with uncertainty. Would he be ok? Would he die? Would he ever be the same? How long would it be? At that point I felt so scared and alone that I broke down and began to sob uncontrollably. During my fits of sobbing I was praying to God to help me get through this. It was then that I had the feeling of someone embracing me. At first I was shocked because I automatically knew who it was. God was with me. After that I was able to calm down and get some rest. I heard and saw nothing that night, but there is no doubt in my mind that during my greatest time of need, I felt God's presence. God was there as always.

Anonymous, Carthage, New York

SEPTEMBER 28

Prayer of a parent for the college application process

God, I am overwhelmed . . . by the brochures that come in the mail,
    not to speak of the financial aid applications.
I am worried about how much pushing I should do about SATs and grades.
    When is it healthy nudging and when is it my need to achieve?
I am concerned about college visits—how many? how far away?
    Can I possibly be impartial?
I feel like an awful nag about references and essays . . . who's going to
    college anyway?

I desperately want my child to have an exciting senior year—
    not focused just on the future but on the accomplishments
    of many years of hard work.
And, most of all, I'm having trouble thinking about letting go
    and seeing this child (this young adult) leave the nest.
    My mouth affirms independence, but my heart says, "my baby."
God, keep me balanced, wise, and willing to expose the fact that I'm human.
Remind me (let me listen when he or she reminds me)—
    that it's not about me. Amen.

SEPTEMBER 29

Rosh Hashanah

They say that the apple we eat is for wholeness and growth,
They say the honey we dip in is for sweetness in our lives.
Please G-d, help me to accomplish these things.
We will toss away our sins at Tashlic to start the year anew,
We will blow the shofar to rejoice in our existence.
Please G-d, help me to reach that time.
I can stand enveloped in love,
I can sing and be thankful,
I can pray for their health, our hope, and an everlasting peace.
Please G-d, help me to see that day.

Sarah Fineberg-Lombardi

SEPTEMBER 30

Lifesaver

Hold me close
Wipe away my tears
Until the sun rises
Over the hill again
I pretend to be strong
I don't know what strength
Is or what anything is anymore.
Because I'm falling
Falling
Falling
Wrap your arms around me
And hold me so close that
I can hear your heartbeat
In my ear
Make me forget everything
Forget my tears
Forget everything except you
Except you
Look into my eyes
Under the sky that's filled
With fragments of fading stars
And keep me close to you
Close to you and
Look into my eyes
Until you forget what
Color they are and you
Can see my soul and
Love me
Fall in love with me
Hold me close
Wipe away my tears
Until the sun
Rises over the hill again.

Antoinette Pudvah

ROOM FOR YOUR THOUGHTS

October

The Fall

It's when the leaves turn orange, red, and yellow.
The cool breezes finally creep out from their summer hibernation.
Some animals become less visible,
Such as the mosquito that annoyed us.
But some animals leave the fall,
Like the geese that disturb
The previously silenced sky.
All of this is your work,
You created this beautiful wonderland.
You blow the leaves off the trees
With your cool breath.
You are the honking in the gray sky.
You made fall a warning for the long winter ahead.
Fall is a time for gathering,
Not just for squirrels and bears,
But for humans, a time for gathering.
Gathering even more love that you have expressed
Through the beautiful Vermont foliage.

Now that we must put the summer behind us,
And spot the winter ahead.
You have made another beautiful fall . . .
And you'll do it again next year.

Alex Campos

OCTOBER 2

Autumn

Autumn now is here
Leaves are changing color fast.
Thanks for the beauty,
O Lord.
Leaves are dancing in the breeze
Thank you, O Lord
Amen.

Gretchen Singer and Sarah Heath-Howe

OCTOBER 3

O gracious God, I saw you yesterday in the pink-orange sun setting in the periwinkle sky. I felt you the other day as I walked down the street and the music from my headphones fit the moment perfectly and magically. I saw you this morning as I was driving and the Sunday morning sun hit my face over the fall trees as I turned the corner. I heard you last night in the music my boyfriend and I listened to and in the way the cool night wind rustled through the trees and crickets made music for the fireflies to dance to. You are all around me, Lord, in all of my senses. In the laughter of my friends, in the songs we sing for you, in the smell of red and orange leaves freshly fallen in yet another autumn season, in the comforting embrace of a trusted adult, in the feeling I get knowing that I have people around me who love me and are there for me, just like you always are. Thank you Lord, for your wonderful creations. Amen.

Sarah Fitzpatrick

OCTOBER 4

Pause for Psalms—Psalm 145

Read Psalm 145.

What is the mood or tone of this psalm? What feelings are expressed? Do you understand the person who wrote this psalm? Can you identify a popular song, movie, or television show in which these emotions are explored? Choose a single verse or line from this psalm and spend some quiet time reflecting on it . . . or simply repeat it over and over again. Create your own words for this psalm. Here is one contemporizing of it.

Psalm 145

Picking up the fallen,
you unbend the spines
of crouching ones.

Every day I will bless you.

Food in starvation
the meat eater and the vegan—
your hand opens.

Every day I will bless you.

Tender with our terror,
you affirm our appetites,
attentive to whine.

Every day I will bless you.

You're able to appear
in the guise of every generation—
flapper or rapper.

Every day I will bless you.

You forgive sinners,
and forgive saints . . .
Honor and compassion.

Every day I will bless you.

OCTOBER 5

Prayer for the Down East AIDS Network Walk

Dear God,
We're walking for people who need our help.
Step by step, all around town we walk with
old folks and kids,
families and grandparents,
singles and doubles, and many dogs, too.
Please let it be sunny and let the walk go well.
Today, we walk for people with AIDS and HIV.

We're sorry that so many people have AIDS.
We wish there were a cure.
We pray that someday, a cure will be found.
Someday there will be a cure,
and people will survive this illness.

We ask that you
help and comfort the people who have AIDS and HIV.
Help them to get better so they may live their lives in peace
without having to worry about their health.
We pray these people will live long and happy lives.

Bless this walk and everyone here today.
Amen.

Youth Fellowship/Confirmation Group
Center Street Congregational Church, UCC, Machias, Maine

OCTOBER 6

Dear God,
Be with me and help me through this test today. Guide my hands to the
answers and help me to remember the answers that I studied. Amen.

Meghan Krato

OCTOBER 7

Stretch Marks
(for Hilary)

The moment she dangles
Into your life from a blue cord,
You know she'll dangle out again,
Leaving holes in the tulip bed
She weeded at four.

You'll find she's pulled stitches
From the hem of your life at eight; you'll wish,
In her thirteenth year, you'd laid a no-wax
Floor down in your heart.

So it's no surprise, one freshman evening,
To come home to outgrown notches
On hope's doorframe; to find she's left echoes,
In the stairwell, of her name;
An empty carton in the frigidaire;
And lights on all over
Your soul.

J. J. Hunt (adult)

OCTOBER 8

Stupid
Aptitude
Tests
single out the worst aspect of education

Silly
Arrogant
Test givers
suppose a child's worth is measured by a number

Scary how much depends on one test
Appalling how it taints people's lives
Terrible how we've come to believe that a
single score can shape our faith, hopes, and dreams

OCTOBER 9

Solitary October

I feel like the only one on this campus
Who has faith in the son of man
All of their actions are immoral
Every conversation I have brings me away from you
Please give me the strength to rise above
To not be changed by them
And to whole-heartedly seek you
Help me to find fellowship among others who know you are God
I know they are out there
Somewhere in all those dorms

Greg Kelley

OCTOBER 10

Yom Kippur

Adonai,
Forgive me for my sins.
For those I did willingly
And those I was too blind to see.
Forgive me for the wrongs I did not right
For the broken pieces I did not mend
And for the damaged things I did not save
Allow me to atone
For sins against those I love
For those whom I did not acknowledge
And for those whom I can no longer apologize to.

Sarah Fineberg-Lombardi

OCTOBER 11

O God, I pray so many things . . . from the small to the great: I pray that I will make a whole bunch of paper airplanes . . . so I can give them to peo-ple. I pray that Bryan will have God in his life. I pray that the war ends. I pray that my Dad will take me to the pumpkin festival. I pray that I don't get cancer or any of these other things I hear about—ruptured aorta, Parkinson's, arthritis, diabetes, brain damage. I pray for safety. Amen.

Ryan Fletcher

OCTOBER 12

For those we destroyed

We know Columbus,
an intrepid explorer,
killed more than he saved.

No modern-day saint
or savior to be found here
in this man's story.

Only tragedy
for those Native people found
and destroyed by him.

His greed overcame
all his good intentions—
we shouldn't celebrate.

Instead, pray for life
lost to all good intentions—
for our forgiveness.

OCTOBER 13

Body Scan

My head feels understanding
My eyes feel clarity
My mouth feels truth
My arms feel strength
My hands feel connection

My heart feels compassion
My back feels stability
My legs feel motivation
My feet feel grounded
My spirit feels open
My soul feels vulnerable
I feel alive.
I hope everyone can feel this alive.

Scott Scaffidi

OCTOBER 14

Adult's prayer for adolescents choosing ministry as a vocation

God, I pray today that you stir a call in the spirits, hearts, minds of young people. Place the hope within that they can preach and pray, marry and bury, visit in the hospital and the home. Let them desire to tell children's sermons, sleep on the floor with youth groups, and think up neat ideas for newsletters.

At church camp or retreat, on the van coming home from a mission trip, or at a career fair at the local high school, even on a Sunday morning so perfectly ordinary that nobody else realizes you are up to a miracle, touch a life with a crazy, amazing, ridiculous recognition—"God is calling me to be a pastor. God is calling **me** to be a pastor."

And then, O God, when some young man or woman responds somewhere deep inside, "Here I am," stir up the rest of us to extend the emotional, psychological, spiritual, and financial support to sustain your call into a grace-filled reality. We pray through the Spirit, which makes every gifted work a ministry. Amen.

O C T O B E R   1 5

Another Autumn Poem

The leaves are crisp
The air is fresh
The smell of chimney smoke is in the air
It ain't too hot nor too cold
Perhaps a swell time to worship the unseen

Greg Kelley

O C T O B E R   1 6

Bible Study—Two Siblings

Read Luke 15:11–32 (this is a parable, a fictional story that Jesus told to make a point)

1) To which of these two characters—the older or the younger child—do you relate?

2) Do you think the parent in the story was fair?

3) If a church youth group is the older sibling, who in your world would be the younger one . . . kids who use drugs, cheat, are in trouble . . . ? If those kids, who had never been a part of the church, were welcomed to a huge Halloween party while the youth group members were expected to rake leaves for all the shut-ins in the congregation, how would the youth group feel?

PRAYER: God, sometimes I feel like the runaway, out-of-control, self-destructive prodigal and sometimes I feel like the critical, full-of-myself, hard-working star student. I always need your love and I always need to share it. Amen.

O C T O B E R   1 7

A Certain Stench: a Taoist's look at cows

With the wind it blows—
a stench so foul
it is a wonder the smell
does not bother the cows—
and we are tried mightily.

We are all tried,
for at times,
there is the need for hamburger.
It is at this point
that the very odor must be accepted,
enjoyed even.

Sam Roden

OCTOBER 18

A Fall Leaf

Gold, more golden than the purest gold.
Or red, each a small flame, burning high in a tree.
Orange, who cannot make up its mind; almost yellow, and almost red.
Tan, unlike the others, is already dead, but still beautiful.
Brown, the final result of each, tumbles along the leaf-strewn ground.

Brendan McCann

OCTOBER 19

ain't much use

i know. i know it ain't the same.
i know. i ain't like them.
sorry if i ain't a user, abuser, manipulator.
sorry if i dunno how to lie.
sorry if i wanna hold you when you cry.
but there ain't much i can do to change for you.
and i ain't about to even if i could.
so take me as i am.
take my words as they are.
i ain't about to lie.
there ain't no use anymore.
no point in tryin' to steal your heart.
there ain't much left.
but it means more to me than anything else.
but it ain't nuthin' unless it's given.

J. S. Price

OCTOBER 20

Heavenly God,
Give me strength as I play in the game today. Help me to fulfill my goals
and give 110%. Give me the courage not to get down on myself or become
frustrated. Help me to play to the best of my ability. Hold my teammates in
your hands and help them to understand the things I am praying to you
now. Most importantly, remind me that playing hard and learning from my
mistakes is more important than winning. Amen.

Liana Merrill

OCTOBER 21

The Phone Number

When I was born
        3-2639
 rang our family home
 connected family news
from Spartanburg
       to Union and Aiken
where my father and mother's families lived

Right after I was old enough
       to learn my phone number
  a longer prefix was added

583-2639
    brought the news that
      of a grandfather's death
        a grandmother's illness
  a sister's baby born

I called that number over the years
    from college
      from naval service in Okinawa
 from my own children's birth rooms

I was called from that number
        when my mother died
    I called it to tell of my divorce;
        called it again when I remarried

The area code changed
    from 803 to 864
the number remained
        linking me to my aging father who lived alone

I called from Rhode Island
                from Massachusetts
            from Maryland
Like an anchor or tethering point
        that number
583-2639
        held me bound to my family
    sometimes in love
                sometimes in anger
    sometimes in deep sadness and concern

My brother called from that number
        to say my father had been hospitalized
            after a fall
        and would not return home
    At 90 he waits in a nursing home
        for his last call

I called it one last time
        864-583-2639
    "We're sorry,
        you have reached a number
            that has been disconnected
    or is no longer in service"

Somewhere
            a line broke free
    and I was adrift

Stephen Price (adult)

OCTOBER 22

On an Amtrak train in upstate New York, sunset

The train rumbles, light vibration
Stone blue silhouette of the Adirondacks
Lining the base of the silver-blue-baby-yellow-and-pink sunset
So close to the Hudson
And its watercolor impression of the winter afternoon
It appears that we are skidding, flying
Just above the river;
It's rush hour,
Simple as the wind moving the water in little ripples
As each toll taken by the railroad rubbles
Which cause every single clack and clink
We float
Under a bridge,
Along the water . . .
Flowing south.

Dag Shaw

OCTOBER 23

We are together
and happy forever.

We eat this food
and if we could
we would
show you our good.

Our God is with us
even on the bus
because God loves us
very, very much.

When we are done
we have fun
because of God.

Diane Hodge

OCTOBER 24

I Want to Live

Stand back, take a seat,
in wonderment.
Our lives, spread out on the table,
our expensive sins.
Hold the hand of each other and make a wish,
I want to live.

Whisper slowly every prayer you need to say.
Let the faith, the beauty of perfect love,
guide your way.
Or scream it from the mountains,
scream it to the oceans,
of the breaking day, and say . . .

Chorus:
I want to live,
I want to live,
I want to live.
Show me how to love.
Show me how to live.
Show me how to be.

Bend your knee, and bow to the beauty of the day.
Crown the king of angels as your eternal way.
Lay down your life, live for your neighbor,
And learn how to pray, and say . . .

Chorus

Abigail Reichard

CTOBER 25

Firm Against the Waves

(dedicated to E. Clifton Baker)
Hold steady to the anchor,
for life's a rolling sea.
I wish I had direction to know,
what is best for me.

Do I have an anchor?
Yes! On my knees to pray.
Making minutes worthwhile,
the best of every day.

I've found a place deep in my heart,
to lay my worries to rest.
God is listening to my prayers,
doing what is best.

With God the sailing is smooth,
you glide right through your life.
I've found my anchor to hold onto,
amidst my troubles and strife.

Rachel Baker

OCTOBER 26

One More

One more moment
that made me think
it was a hopeless fight.
One more moment
You pulled me through;
I can survive anything with you

One more moment
that made me wonder
how long could I possibly last?
One more moment
You proved to me
Your promise is steadfast.

My words cannot attempt to try
to express your power, your strength,
Your all-consuming fire,
Your might, your height,
Your length, your depth,
Your love.

Annie Lalish

OCTOBER 27

Pumpkin

A pumpkin,
a symbol of fall
growing in the field.
A face on halloween
glowing in the night.
A loaf of bread
fresh from the oven,
a pie made for Thanksgiving—
a pumpkin.

Brendan McCann

OCTOBER 28

Prayer of an Adult before a Mission Trip or Service Project

God, forgive me for praying in this order *my* needs.

Let this experience be both fun and fulfilling so that
the kids connect helping others with a great time
and life-changing personal satisfaction.
Keep us safe in travel and free from inner-group conflicts.
Please don't let the innocence, ignorance, or thoughtlessness
of our young people result in inappropriate comments
about situations that may be new to them.
Open all our hearts (young and old) to new neighbors,
especially ones who are unfamiliar, maybe frightening.

May this participation in helping others nurture
not only charity but also a passion for justice
and a desire to shape the future
so that mission work will be obsolete. Amen.

OCTOBER 29

Autumn Wonderland

As I walk through the leaves, I sigh as I remember that this autumn won-derland will soon be strewn with snow and frost. The autumn is the best time—with its crunch of leaves and all of its golden splendor. As autumn dies in the turn of the seasons, it lives on in our hearts. As I walk down the hills I look around . . . and realize that autumn is a melancholy season. I watch the trees losing their leaves and the children jumping and burrowing into them. The leaves are scattered and twirl in a gust of wind. I am grow-ing older. I thank the Creator for this season.

Nate Bobowski

OCTOBER 30

Graves are a frightening place to the living.

How do we know what happens after we are put in the ground.

Often, we tell ghost stories—is that how we'll all end up?

Some hold the belief that people will go to Heaven or Nirvana after
we've passed.

Though others feel there is the potential for reincarnation.

So many possibilities, hopes, and fears exist, yet we will never truly know
until it is our time.

OCTOBER 31

Disguise

If Jesus were here,
what would he wear for Halloween?

He could be a shepherd—
dressed up in his dad's old bathrobe
and carrying his little sister around as a sheep
to be gently prodded up every porch.

He might like to be a teacher—
assigning homework
to those people who give out apples
or toothbrushes instead of candy.

He could be a fisherman—
dragging stinky nets
and throwing fish heads around,
all the while practicing how to walk on water.

If Jesus were here,
would he dress like a hobo
the way my brother does every year?

Maybe so.

Maybe that's been his costume every day
and we've just ceased to recognize the holy in him.

Maria I. Tirabassi

ROOM FOR YOUR THOUGHTS

November

NOVEMBER 1

Gracious and Loving God—
Thank you.
Thank you for loving me as you do.
Thank you for the many blessings
I receive each and every day.
When I am in need, you are there.
When I'm filled with joy, you are there.
Halleluia!
You are my true inspiration—
salvation and glory.
You are my true inspiration—
honor and power.
Yes! You are my true inspiration—
wonderful and merciful.
Halleluia!
Bless, I pray, not only me,
but all of us,
this day and forevermore. Amen.

Dana Baker

NOVEMBER 2

God,

You help us every day to try and eliminate war, hate, and crime. You help us through all the decisions we make, and you don't ask for much in return. Thank you for all you do and I hope you keep on giving. In Jesus' name we pray. Amen.

Vanessa Ruff

NOVEMBER 3

You're OK (Porcelain Doll)

Wipe your eyes hide your tears, and smile
smile 'til it hurts
So they'll think you're ok
and not worry.
Hide your tears and say, "Thank you,"
Again and again
Until it becomes automatic
And the words lose their meaning
So they'll think you're ok
and not worry.
Smile 'til it hurts and your face freezes
your rosy lips in a sugared pose
Forever phrasing a honey, "Thank you,"
Like a doll whose porcelain cheeks are wet.
Become a doll and smile 'til it hurts
So they'll think you're ok
And not worry.
Porcelain is oh so strong and hides its cracks
But even the strongest will bust
If it's dropped
    hard enough
        long enough
and though they'll dismiss the first fissure
when you break
they'll no longer think you're ok
And they will worry.

Gabriele S. Chase

NOVEMBER 4

Thank You, God

O Lord, God, our Salvator, we thank you for all the wonderful blessings that you give us. Please, God, give us strength to be strong enough to do your will. Let the devil's power be weak, for we know, dear God, that you can do all things. You are an awesome God. We thank you for everything. Amen.

Lanetta Blount

NOVEMBER 5

Pause for Psalms—Psalm 35

Read Psalm 35.

What is the mood or tone of this psalm? What feelings are expressed? Do you understand the person who wrote this psalm? Can you identify a popular song, movie, or television show in which these emotions are explored? Choose a single verse or line from this psalm and spend some quiet time reflecting on it . . . or simply repeat it over and over again. Create your own words for this psalm. Here is one contemporizing of it.

Psalm 35

I wept for them;
I prayed for them;
I worried when they were sick, hurt,
depressed—
but, when it happened to me,
they flocked to the smell
of blood.
They enjoyed my misfortune;
they tasted my shame,
my hurt . . .
with relish.

So let them be
windblown sage brush.
Let their way be dark and slippery,
and, when they are already lost,
send scary angels
to chase them down.

NOVEMBER 6

The First Tuesday in November

Election Day smells of scandal
and recounts, of impeachment threats,
of war,
a blue dress and the middle east in flames.
It reeks of anticipated deception,
patriotism, resentment—
of disappointment in the definition of democracy.

We choose to believe
in slick lies—not because they go down easy,
or because we sleep better at night—
but because we hope for truth in disguise.

We miss our faith in leaders
and optimistic flag-waving—
we remember childhood's easy answers.

We want to be proud
in a country that once offered
nothing but a promise of beginnings,
a land that used to provide endless opportunity.

We ask, on this day, for our faith
to be rewarded,
and our trust redeemed
by those who are chosen to lead.

Anonymous, Boston, Massachusetts

NOVEMBER 7

Prayer for the treatment of a juvenile sex offender

He used to be a Victim
    small and vulnerable to the blows
        of belt and extension cord that striped his body
Powerless against the sexual urges
    of mother and her boyfriends
        that scarred his soul and psyche.

Now he's learned
    that Power can be gained
        by "doing unto others what was once done to you"
So other children fear him
        while the courts call him a Predator
           a Monster
               a Serial Rapist in Training
And they send him to us for "treatment." Now he's on my caseload.

O God
    Help me hold
His past in one hand
        And his growing violent present/future in the other
 Help us find healing for him together
           Before the past and future nail him to a rigid life
of violence, pain,
    rape, and murder.
And the cross he's nailed to becomes a stake driven into the heart of the world.

Stephen Price (adult)

NOVEMBER 8

Tiny Flame

Silent Serenity
Darkened room
Tiny flame
Shines out from the gloom
All are gathered
'Round a bin of sand
All have a candle
In their own hand.
Tiny flame
Moves from one hand to another
And in each hand
It creates its own brother.
Many tiny flames
Move about the room
Many tiny flames
Can't penetrate the gloom.
Tiny flame
Moves toward the center.
Tiny flame
From the hand of a repenter.
Placed in the sand
Tiny flame does stay.
Tiny flame in the center
Creates a tiny ray.
But when joined by others,
Tiny flame does grow.
Tiny flames in the center
Joined in a row.
Tiny flames shining brightly
So all can see
When all join together
Look what we can be!

Brianna Chamberlain

NOVEMBER 9

I read somewhere that people always turn to God to ask for things they need or want but that they seldom give thanks for the things they have received. But that is my favorite thing to pray:

Thank you, God, for giving me my optimism. Thanks for making me who I am. Thank you for helping me weather the storms you've sent and emerge safely on the other side. I'm glad I'm a happy person. I believe that everything will be okay . . . everything, all situations. Maybe it's residual naïveté from my childhood, but I kind of like it. If I wasn't so happy I think it would be more difficult to find particular things to be thankful for. Giving thanks lightens my heart and spirit—and I'm happy. Then I'm grateful for that! It's a beautiful circle.

Courtney Randall

NOVEMBER 10

All loving God, please be with us as we go about our daily lives so caught up with this material world. Help us to find your presence and live our lives in love. Please assist us in appreciating the true beauty of this world you have given us. Amen.

Gretchen Andrus and Laura Fries

NOVEMBER 11

A young liberal celebrates Veterans' Day

God, I've always respected my grandfathers
for fighting the battles they have,
in claiming peace could be found
through violence—
but times were different back in their day.

The wars they fought had a certain necessity,
and to take up your place on the front line,
that was a choice kids could believe in.

For my own friends though,
I can't understand why they'd enlist.
The glory has gone out of even the idea of war
and all I can think about is the games
we used to play together as children.

It wasn't so long ago
we were scrambling to wash up for dinner,
and yet, they've become veterans at twenty-one.

They're strangers to me,
men and women who have seen death too often
for me to imagine;
and it makes me wonder—
if I had known my grandfathers
before they had taken medals and folded flags,
would they have been strange to me too?

NOVEMBER 12

God, we come to you today hoping you will accept our thanks and praises
and grant our prayers. God, we thank you for this day and for helping us
through this beautiful day. We thank you for sending your son, Jesus
Christ, to forgive our many sins that we so thoughtlessly committed. We
pray for those who are sick, stressed, or have lost a loved one. God, hear
our prayers. Amen.

Anonymous #2, Owensville, Missouri

NOVEMBER 13

I am going to die.

That's what I've decided
since I haven't studied for my SATs
and they're tomorrow morning.

I don't think I've ever dreaded Saturday so much in my life.

All my friends took prep classes.
I didn't.

My teachers offered tips.
I wasn't listening.
Even my parents had suggestions for vocabulary to review.
I didn't care.

But I care now!!!
Please please please let it be easier than everyone says.
I don't know what I'll do when I get to that math section,
but I'm pretty sure I'm doomed.
(To be honest,
I don't even know what a graphing calculator
is supposed to do.)

If I survive this . . .
I have to survive this . . .
maybe it won't be so bad.

Or maybe it will.

I know this isn't really the right reason to pray,
but
please please please God . . .

help.

Ingrid, Somerville, Massachusetts

NOVEMBER 14

Prayer of a Chemistry Teacher

There is a wonderful moment when you see that a young person has grasped something new. In chemistry I ask students to understand concepts they cannot see. They must gain their insights regarding an invisible world through metaphors and models. Attempts to express new ways of seeing, whether through art, music, poetry, math, or technology, only succeed when another connects with those ideas or insights. "I get it!" need not be shouted, it is written on the face. To be a part of their "ah-ha" is a blessing.

Robert Young

NOVEMBER 15

God, these November days are quiet and peaceful and feel almost like holding their breath before the excitement of the holidays. I love this dark time. I walk through the park with my small dog kicking dried leaves, umber and maroon ones, crisp. When I turn back the light in my home reminds me of family warmth for which I am most grateful when I am chilled by the wind blowing. I remember that there are others who cannot be inside. In this autumn reverie expand my heart to include the homeless. Amen.

Anonymous, Des Moines, Iowa

NOVEMBER 16

Bible Study—Esther

You may want to read through the book of Esther (which is short). If you don't have that much time, be sure to read 2:1–11; 4:4–14; 7:1–10.

1) Esther used her attractiveness and sexuality to save her people from massacre. Have you ever consciously used your appearance or changed your behavior to impress someone or further your goals? If so, how did it make you feel?

2) Esther made a devious plan to save the Jewish people. Can you relate to that experience?

3) Choosing between personal security and comfort and helping many people (or one other person) is difficult. Have you ever recognized that dilemma (or do you now)?

PRAYER: God, each of us is born into "such a time as this." Let me recognize how I might help others and what gifts I have that I can use for your purpose in my time. Amen.

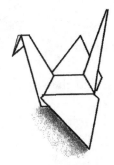

NOVEMBER 17

Crane

For Nan Gertz

You're
Graceful, Elegant,
Beautiful, Serene.
My Friend and My Light.
You're
Strong, Valiant,
Sage, True.
My Help, My Guide
My Crane.

Genevieve Bergeron

NOVEMBER 18

Sometimes life isn't fair
Every kid knows that is the truth
We don't get our way

When life is unfair
It's hard for us understand
Why life goes this way

We learn in time though
Every cloud has its lining
We will have our day

NOVEMBER 19

Thanking You

We give thanksgiving for all that is great.
In your hands we leave our fate.
Thankful for life, family, friends, and the seas,
Every detail to the tranquil breeze.
Thanking you, thanking you.
We should be thanking you.

Here we are learning together, working together,
Praying together as one,
We thank you, O God, for our happiness.
We look to you for our strength and greatness,
Grateful for all the things we have gained,
Giving thanks for the hope that our families attained—
Thanking you, thanking you.
We should be thanking you. Amen.

Sira Grant

NOVEMBER 20

Morning Prayer

I pray in the morning for the children who don't have a
bed to pray on at night;
I pray that all people be kind to one another;
I pray that I won't be greedy because I know
that I already have a lot that some people don't have;
I pray that God is with me to help me be special in a person's life,
which might not be as wonderful as mine.
And I pray for the thanks in me to let God know
just how wonderful my life is!

Molly Weston

NOVEMBER 21

Litany for teens in many kinds of families

God, we pray for our young people in their many different families.

RESPONSE: *Here are my mother and father, sister and brother.*
Whoever does the will of God is my family (Mark 3:34–5, adapted)

We pray for teenagers in multigenerational families.
RESPONSE

We pray for teenagers in blended families.
RESPONSE

We pray for families in which the gender orientation
of parent or child is an ongoing issue.
RESPONSE

We pray for single-parent households.
RESPONSE

We pray for young people in lonely apartments (chosen or not).
RESPONSE

We pray for college roommates.
RESPONSE

We pray for teenagers in intimate commitments—
some publicly acknowledged and some not.
RESPONSE

We pray for families where death has left a mark this year.
RESPONSE

We pray for families in crisis, especially the crisis of domestic violence.
RESPONSE

We pray for foster families.
RESPONSE

We pray for the relationship between birth parents
and adoptive parents and the children they nurture.
RESPONSE

We pray for families reconstituted the first year after divorce.
RESPONSE

We pray for this church family and the way it enfolds everyone with love.
RESPONSE

Anonymous (adult)

NOVEMBER 22

God, you are the Creator of many great works.
Your unique style is reflected through music.
Your thoughts, ideas, and inspirations are evident in every piece,
though each piece is unique and different.
A composer's own style exists through many elements.
You, oh God, are our composer—
you create the music of our lives.
But we aren't your masterpiece . . .
we, as Christians, are your musicians.
We live our lives with our own creative style—
always following the notes that you create for us. Amen.

Erin Newcomb

NOVEMBER 23

I pray for:
   My grandfather, who is experiencing Alzheimer's.
   My friends, who are always there for me.
   My brother, who always has kind and comforting words to share.
   My mom and dad, who have guided me through life and helped me
       over hurdles I've come across.
   The children in Iraq and other children in need.
   People who have fought in war and kept hope alive.
   Forgiveness from God and thankfulness for all wonderful creations
       he has made.
   Peace on Earth.
   A solution to world hunger and cancer.
   The Boston Red Sox!
   Everyone on Earth who needs a little light and guidance from God.

Anonymous, Melrose, Massachusetts

NOVEMBER 24

A Thanksgiving Prayer

On this day it is right to give thanks to God.
Whether we celebrate all together, with a large or small family,
whether we sit in solitude or eat a simple meal,
whether our family has been apart or has stayed together,
whether we celebrate life or mourn death,
whether we cannot afford enough to feed our family,
even if we have no food at all.

To understand these circumstances
is to come to terms with the world we live in.

It is important to understand that,
while there may be plenty to curse,
today is a day of peace; a day for remembrance;
a day for loving ourselves and others—
more than those close to us or those we've just met . . .
humankind, big and small, far and near, young and old alike.

Share your compassion with others,
and watch the chain of giving expand,
creating more love, providing a sense of serenity.
Today on Thanksgiving, we pray for hope—
hope for everyone,
the light of hope shining on all people.

Olin Johannessen

NOVEMBER 25

God bless America
   and the sick
      and the starving
         and the poor
  and the disheartened
      and the landless
   and the homeless
  and the weak
     and the oppressed

and those who cry out
    and those who have no voice . . .
. . . inside this country and without,
for sorrow knows no boundaries—
    no lines of race or creed or religion or ethnicity
        or gender or sexual preference or economic status
            or nationality or living conditions—
but neither does compassion.
Hate can arise anywhere, but it sees only the boundaries,
    the black and white,
        the "us" and "them."
Love likewise springs up anywhere, but there are no limits,
    no marks of distribution or quantity,
for Love is transcending
    and surpassing
        and infinite.

Gabriele S. Chase

NOVEMBER 26

I thank you, God, for:
My loving family,
My wonderful friends,
A great city and neighborhood,
A good education,
The things I have that are priceless,
That make my life the great thing it is.

Sarah Whisnant

NOVEMBER 27

A Prayer for the Hungry

I pray for those starving in China
And those without food in Peru
But also I pray for my high school
Because people are starving here too

I pray for those crying from hunger
The children who cry out in fear
And also I pray for the girls that I know
Who cry when they look in the mirror

I pray for the millions who never have food
The famines I see in the news
And also I pray for my friends at my school
Because hunger is something they choose

I pray for the boy with just one cup of rice
and the thin girl I see at the mall
I pray for them both to have something to eat
For they aren't much different at all

So pray for the starving in China
And pray for the girls whose dreams are unreal
Pray that they both will never again
Have to suffer from skipping a meal

Rachel Northrop

NOVEMBER 28

Adult's Prayer for the Lonely Kid in the Library

God, I have felt like that young person looks, alone in the same seat in the library every afternoon. I really don't know why he sits there—whether he's an outcast from the popular group, seeking refuge from an angry home, or just cramming a high school project into a short time. Whatever it is, I see the slump of the shoulders, the droop at the corner of the mouth—and I remember all sorts of lonely moments that were a part of my adolescence. Whenever this young person or any other feels that sadness, God, send an angel, or even better . . . send a friend. Amen.

NOVEMBER 29

This was written after a meteor shower while camping on Mount Shasta. According to a family on a farm in Washington, very close to the borders of Idaho and Canada, "caspers" are unexpected spheres of glowing light that occur mysteriously on their property, formerly the land of Kalispel Indians. These caspers are known to be harmless and have followed people through the property before. In the two or three months I was there, though, I did not see one.

I remember the first snow I saw fall this year
the sky was full of pinholes and a meteor shower glowed on us down here
And I watched the comets mingle with the stars
Like whirlwinds of snowflakes
Whirring around.

In the still headlights
I stared through the windshield.
There were sparkles like glitter
Like St. Elmo's Fire
Like jaspars . . . the caspers I've come to expect . . .
But then I saw a downward fleck of white
A little icy streak of light
Shooting stars that pile like a marshmallow ground . . .
Silent like little magic spirits gather.

Dag Shaw

NOVEMBER 30

This life is a gift—and everything in it.
Do I appreciate it?
How fragile is this life? How rare is it?
What do I have? Make no comparisons with anyone.
Have I taken more than I need?
What do I have to give?
Whom do I have to thank?

Before you go out into public, look at your soul in the mirror.
Forgive yourself. Do this before anything else.

Don't continue until you can do this.

Be comfortable with yourself.
Be honest to yourself.
Confide in yourself.
Love yourself.

If you can do all of this, recognize your strength,
your will, your life and beauty.
The greatest challenge is always
within. When you can confront yourself,
your life will be your dream,
and when we share this dream, our world will be our heaven.

Anonymous, Ojai, California

ROOM FOR YOUR THOUGHTS

December

DECEMBER 1

The band plays on

We wear little red ribbons
one day a year
for the infants in Africa—
one out of every four
(if the statistics can be believed)—
tiny bodies struggling
without our prayers.

Yes, those little red ribbons
remind us of the crisis
in the eighties,
of the gay community
crying out collectively for some cure,
some solution to prolong death,
without our support.

Coat labels sport little red ribbons
for the quiet graves
born of an unmentionable disease—

an illness we ignore
in favor of newer sleek
killers that come unguarded against
without our acceptance.

Little red ribbons are not enough—
not without
our prayers,
our support,
our refusal to accept
death
with a thousand faces.

Ingrid, Somerville, Massachusetts

DECEMBER 2

The Coming of Christmas

The first snowflake falls onto the icy ground,
The Lord watches as winter creeps around,
The days grow shorter and the nights seem longer,
The season for love and giving grows stronger,
Soon Christmas arrives as snow fills all sight,
Time slowly passes as Jesus shines his Holy Light,
Families gather to bow their heads in prayer,
Thanking the Lord for all his love and care.

Kariann Bergman

DECEMBER 3

Thanksgiving prayer while skiing

When you're hurtling down the face of a mountain strapped to a pair of boards, it's hard to devote a part of your thoughts to much beyond where your next turn will be and how sharp you can make it without sailing into the trees.

That's not where I am right now.

At the top of the summit on a bluebird day, a sensation of freedom over-whelms me and at that moment—the second I feel that all ties are severed, I feel compelled to turn and thank someone. So thank you. I could have been anyone. I could have been anywhere else. Trite as it all looks now on paper, thank you for making me all that I am. Thank you for creating all the beauty that surrounds me; thank you for giving me the senses with which to appreciate your work and your power and your majesty.

And I think all this as I contemplate which trail to take; I retain that feeling of awe in your power as I begin my descent. Thank you, God.

Courtney Randall

DECEMBER 4

Advent is a time for quiet reflection.

During these weeks, we ask God for blessings on our families and friends.

Very soon, Christmas will come and we will celebrate Christ's birth in that chaos.

Everyone has this period to do good for others and remember what the season is truly about.

Nothing is more important than celebration and joy within ourselves and with others.

Take a moment to rejoice during this month and always.

DECEMBER 5

Pause for Psalms—Psalm 51

Read Psalm 51.

What is the mood or tone of this psalm? What feelings are expressed? Do you understand the person who wrote this psalm? Can you identify a popular song, movie, or television show in which these emotions are explored? Choose a single verse or line from this psalm and spend some quiet time re-flecting on it . . . or simply repeat it over and over again. Create your own words for this psalm. Here is one contemporizing of it.

Psalm 51

This I ask of God—
mercy in spite of my sins,
a bent spirit whole.

This I fear from God—
a face of disappointment,
repentance refused.

This I seek from God—
laundered heart and sweet spirit,
cold and clean as snow.

This I give to God—
a broken and contrite heart,
hardest gift to give.

This I speak for God—
"justice, peace, and tenderness,
are freely offered."

DECEMBER 6

An Advent Blessing

In this time of Advent, we remember the birth of our Savior and the Spirit within us all. The spirit to strive for humanity, compassion, and kindness. The spirit to be considerate of one another in every season, not just now. Thank you for this reminder, for the birth of Jesus into our lives and our hearts. As we sing carols, provide us with new meaning for us. Not just familiar words, but new words in our hearts. Guide us to be moved by the spirit we feel now, O God, and throughout the year. Amen.

Katherine Spain

DECEMBER 7

Prayer of a Youth Group Leader

Gracious, Loving God full of wisdom, mercy, and grace, thank you for guiding me into the lives of young people and empowering me with the strength and conviction to model to my youth groups the ways in which we can be as you expect: humble, helpful, and understanding without prejudice.

Please keep a watchful eye over our youth groups and their mission work and help us to succeed in your divine plan. Remind us of your presence and forgive us when we think that what we do is totally us. We need your guidance in all that we do and all that we do is truly in your name. Amen.

Sheila J. Rizzotti, Danvers, Massachusetts

DECEMBER 8

Dear God,
Why is the train always late when I need to get to class on time? Is that really necessary, or is it more of a quirk in Fate's design that keeps life from getting too dull? You see, I really don't understand why it should happen so often—I mean, when I'm early, I never have any problems at all. So why me? Why should I be made to suffer this injustice on a daily basis? Isn't it enough that I occasionally try to help others (you know, when it's convenient for me and my schedule) and that I can sometimes spare a buck for that guy who stinks of piss and whisky who lives on on the corner of Brookline and Green St.? Don't I do my part by sharing only the most interesting of my friends' secrets instead of gossiping about everything that happens in their lives? Or what about how I've really cut back on lying, you know, except for when the truth would hurt somebody's feelings or put me out? I think I deserve a little more from your end—when will you start pulling your weight in this relationship?
Sincerely,
an irate citizen

Dear Irate Citizen,
At the risk of sounding preachy, I think you need to reexamine your life before you complain to me about the train schedule and your "rights," as you see them.
Nowhere is it written "life is fair"—if you don't believe me, ask the kids growing up in Israel or Palestine or Iraq or . . . well, pretty much anywhere in Africa where the

AIDS epidemic is killing more people everyday than you'll probably meet in your entire life. Check out the situation in Somalia or Afghanistan and tell me you aren't the lucky one. If you can't take time out of that busy schedule, look around you and see the fear and anger and tragedy reflected in the eyes of too many you love. Doesn't that make you think it's possible that there's more to life than punctuality? With eternal and forgiving love,
God

Anonymous, Cambridge, Massachusetts

DECEMBER 9

Reason for the Season

Dear God, thank you for the Christmas holidays, for the birth of your Son, Jesus. Help us not to forget that he came from heaven to earth to save us all from aimlessness and to forgive us for our sins. Help us, O God, to remember the importance of this season is to praise you for Jesus' birth. I hope and pray that on this day of Christ's birth we all become humble to your will and your way. Also, O God, I would like to remember the homeless, the lonely, and the unfortunate ones who on this day have nothing, and have no hope. Hopefully, they will remember that the life that you've allowed us to live is much more valuable than the things in the world in which we live. God, I thank you for all these blessings you have bestowed upon us. In Jesus' name. Amen

Michelle Brothers

DECEMBER 10

Advent

We wait your coming
The inbreaking of God's love.
Come now.

Andrea Kautz

DECEMBER 11

Father Lord,

Help me, Lord, to be strong, and to walk in the way Jesus taught us. Let me realize that being honest is the only way to be. Help me, Father, not to give in to sin and to know that living the way you want us to isn't easy, but will lead us to your kingdom of righteousness. Let me be thankful, Lord, to reflect on all the blessings I have and be content, rather than reflect on all of the things I don't have and be selfish, knowing that there are others in the world who have much less. Help me, Lord, to bring your word and your light to others who need it.

Help me, LORD, to live like a Christian
    To live like your son JESUS
        Amen.

Astrid Portillo

DECEMBER 12

Advent Grace

Dear Lord, I pray for this food to nourish our bodies.
I thank you for my family's friends.
Thank you for getting everyone here safely and please let everyone get home safely too.
Thank you for the beginning of Advent and for sending your only Son.
Amen.

Melissa Bartlett

DECEMBER 13

God, thank you for those winters that I remember. Thank you for being able to jump into snowbanks, and for sledding down hills. Thank you for this time to get in touch with myself, my friends, my family. Amen.

Johannes Greisshammer

DECEMBER 14

Prayer for Light in a Time of Darkness

As we stand together kindling the Hanukkah candles
We marvel at the light in this time of darkness
Like the Jews of long ago, we find hope in our flames.

Ellen Fineberg (adult)

DECEMBER 15

LEADER: As we celebrate Jesus' birth
PEOPLE: Abide with us, Emmanuel
Leader: As we see the sun shine on the snow
PEOPLE: Abide with us, Emmanuel
Leader: As we enjoy playing or watching basketball
PEOPLE: Abide with us, Emmanuel
Leader: As we light candles to light the way
PEOPLE: Abide with us, Emmanuel
Leader: As we bake cookies with the family
PEOPLE: Abide with us, Emmanuel
Leader: As friends and family gather
PEOPLE: Abide with us, Emmanuel
Leader: As we miss friends from school while on vacation
PEOPLE: Abide with us, Emmanuel
Leader: As we wait for the New Year's coming
PEOPLE: Abide with us, Emmanuel
Leader: As we sing praises this Christmas season
PEOPLE: Abide with us, Emmanuel
Leader: As we have fun decorating trees and houses
PEOPLE: Abide with us, Emmanuel
ALL: Stay with us when Christmas is over. Amen.

Melissa Bartlett, Kristen Toews, and Scott Martin

DECEMBER 16

Bible Study—Mary of Nazareth

Read Luke 1:26–56.

1) Mary was an unwed teenager! In what ways is she a model for your life?

2) What does Mary's song say about social hierarchies? How can you be a part of God's shifting the balance between rich and poor?

3) What have been your experiences with teen pregnancy and its choices—school friends, family, yourself? How do you respond to "Marys" around you?

PRAYER: God, I want to be open to those things that might be born because of my willingness—in my own life, my community, my world. Help me experience the Christmas story with far more intensity than as a greeting card, a pageant, an excuse for presents. Amen.

DECEMBER 17

Friends—what does it mean?
Rely on, believe in,
someone to listen when you need to whine,
someone to help out in a tight spot,
someone to press into labor.
Let them always be there!

Jeannine Karr

DECEMBER 18

We may not have a lot of money for fancy things, but
Love holds our country church together.
We may not have a lot of people for each Sunday, but
Love holds our country church together.
What do we have? A close-knit family believing in God, where
Love holds our country church together.

Maria McLane

DECEMBER 19

Angel Voice

An angel singing
has no words.
She does not need them to tell she is always with you.
Her voice brings you comfort
and stops the crying.
You may hear her faint song
in your head,
but you listen the loudest
in your heart.
When her voice is heard,
you think she is near,
but no matter how far she may be,
she will always touch you
with her wordless song.
She is an angel.

Ashley Schmiedicke

DECEMBER 20

Hanukkah

Nothing permeates a house quite like frying latkes and homemade apple-sauce. The sweet scent of apples and cinnamon blends with the oil and onion and potatoes across the kitchen. And somewhere beneath the cooking smells and the chatter of a family together at a table, is the subtle aroma of melting wax and burning wicks. Candles fill the window, food fills my belly, and when I spend these holidays with my family, warmth fills my heart.

Sarah Fineberg-Lombardi

DECEMBER 21

Christmas Eve prayer of the parent of a twenty-year-old

I want to count this blessing . . .
One night she goes to sleep before I do.
I can kiss her without her knowing.
There are not many years left—
maybe not any—
when she will be in this bed
on Christmas Eve.
I catch my breath, O Mary—
the temporary joy of the manger.

DECEMBER 22

Dear God,
Your joyful child wants to thank you for always being the light of the
world and lighting even the darkest corners of the globe with your unend-
ing love. Please continue to do this and help me keep loving and caring as
you do. Thank you. Amen.

Meghan O'Connor

DECEMBER 23

Help a lucky boy find his way.

When each direction seems okay,
and not one seems to lead astray,
in a rut called paradise,
the middle ground is not the way.

Easier said than done, I say:
help a lucky boy find his way.

On a silver platter I was given
this bountiful world that I live in,
and an appetite for a kingly feast.
Help me share it with the least.

Easier said than done, I say:
help a lucky boy find his way.

Fortunate, aren't we all.
To shop and watch, to type and call,
to eat and sleep, to cook and clean,
to love and learn, to rise and fall.

Like the sun, we shine and stare
at busy planets, unaware
of each one's turn, each day and night
But this I swear, there is a light.

There's a light for every day, and there's a moon for every sun,
and when you follow, light the way, because you revolve around everyone.
Though this mind may spin alone, to each other, let me say,
help me rise, help me rise, help me turn night into day.
Though I may have all the light, a fortunate son would like to say,
rise with me, please rise with me, help me turn night into day.

Easier said than done, I pray,
help a lucky boy find his way.

Anonymous, Ojai, California

DECEMBER 24

Christmas Eve

For as long as I can remember
on the twenty-fourth of December,
my sisters and I would get dressed up nice,
and bake a special something with sugar and spice.
When our baking was done,
off we would run
to Granny and Grandpa's house,
not exactly as quiet as a mouse.
The gifts were piled near the tree.
To the presents ran my cousins and me.
"Not yet, you guys," my mom would say,
so, slowly, with sad faces we'd walk away.

Later what we'd do was this—
we'd break wafers and give each relative a kiss—
then a feast we would eat
where we'd have anything except for meat.
Grandpa said grace
while on the ground Spunky would pace.
Once we were done
back to the presents we would run.
"Hurry up!" we'd cry,
until our parents sat nearby.
Thank you's were shouted and the paper flew
and we were happy till it was time to say to you . . .
"Good night, Merry Christmas, and Happy New Year, too."

Jaclyn Kregling

DECEMBER 25

Christmas

Christ is born to us
He shall be the Prince of Peace
Rejoice!

Andrea Kautz

DECEMBER 26

I don't know the season, God.
I'm bigger than seasons.
I'm inside.
I'm curled up.
I'm thinking.
I'm not speaking.

Matt LaRoche

DECEMBER 27

God, let my parents NOT talk about their sex life. Please! Dear God, it's the greatest fear in a teenager's life. Just let it end! Please! Amen.

Anonymous, Pepperell, Massachusetts

DECEMBER 28

God of the Dead of Winter,
I'm praying now for teenagers I have known who are stuck in the "dead" of winter. And I'm thinking of teenagers all over whom I've never met, who may be feeling cold and lifeless inside right now. God, you know how icy this world can be, and how cold and brittle our hearts can get when the winter winds blow.

But enough of winter metaphors. I want this prayer to be real, stark, severe, and blunt. Like winter itself can be—but there I go again. God, I'm praying for teens whose hearts are broken right now. For kids who wake up to too much anger, too little love, and nothing in the house for breakfast. For teens that aren't sure if anyone really cares about them, or if anyone would even notice if they just didn't show up somewhere today. I'm praying for teens who don't want to be in school, not just because its boring or because there's too much academic pressure. I'm praying for the kids who dread walking through those school doors because someone is probably waiting there to hurt them—physically maybe, but more likely in some emotional way. For the teens who aren't cool. Who don't fit in. Who don't look good or feel good. For the ones who will have all they can handle to just not let it show too much when someone makes fun of them as they walk by. I'm praying for the ones who hate their bodies, who can't get rid of their zits, who aren't very good at anything that seems to matter. I'm praying for the ones who hate lunch because they don't really have anyone to sit with, or at least no one they really could call a friend. I'm praying for the teens who hate Sunday afternoons because it makes them too aware that another Monday is almost there. And for those who also hate Fridays, because the weekend only reminds them of how alone they are.

O God, please help people today who feel stuck in the dead of winter. If someone reading this prayer feels that way right now, then please help that person find a place of warmth today. It doesn't have to be a perfect fire in a fireplace, though that sounds pretty good, but just a little warmth somewhere to remind them that the coldness is not all there is. God, remind someone today that you really do exist. Find a way to show them that your Love is all over the place, even when it seems hidden or far away. And God, if there is a way that I can be a source of your warmth for someone, then please make that happen. Even if things are feeling pretty cold inside me, I'm asking you to wrap me up in blankets of your Love, and to help me notice and respond to others who might need your Love blankets too. Help me to notice those who never get noticed. To say hello to people who don't think I know their names. To invite someone to talk or hang out or sit down with me and my friends, someone who never gets invited. But to do it because I really care, not because I'm trying to be "good" or to make someone feel like my little project. God, be warm in me, and let someone else feel that warmth when they get close to me. In Jesus' name I pray these things. Amen.

Bryan Sirchio (adult)

DECEMBER 29

Pray for love. Pray for joy.
Pray for a friend or a toy and let your body go.
Pray for life. Pray for need.
Pray for actions. Pray for what you preach.

Michael Clark

DECEMBER 30

San Francisco, 1:36 P.M.

The warm sun in December
    Is a miracle to me,
Like the bright purple flowers
    In the park at the end of the street.

Dag Shaw

DECEMBER 31

I find you in focus

I shut my eyes and watch you dance across sparkling lids;
and at the end of the day, I rest my head, knowing you do the same
three thousand miles from my side—your arms enclose me,
hold me snug darkness through dawn.

When day comes, I open my eyes and see your smile in the morning dew,
silver light tingeing blades of grass as the breeze whispers your love
while hazel sighs the azure skies, the brightness of a beating pang—
the pounding of intrepid hearts—

boom. Boom.

We blink in time, a beating pang,
the symphony of a silver dawn.

Anonymous, Cambridge, Massachusetts

ROOM FOR YOUR THOUGHTS

Index of Contributors

Index of Selected Topics